HUNGARIAN
PROVINCIAL COOKING

Júlia Frank

CORVINA

Published by Corvina Books, Ltd.

1072 Budapest, Rákóczi út 16
e-mail: corvina@t-online.hu
www.corvinakiado.hu

ISBN 963 13 5485 7

PREFACE

Dear Reader,

You are holding a special cookbook, with recipes of real Hungarian provincial food. I can already hear the skeptical remarks: Why would we want to read about fattening, unhealthy, out-of-date dishes, let alone eat them?!

It is an understandable question. I can assure you, however, that all the recipes in this book comply with the requirements of healthy nutrition while preserving the traditional flavors of Hungarian peasant food. I included several recipes for simple dishes that Hungarians in the past regularly ate without knowing the health benefits. Some of these dishes have long been forgotten and it is time for them to resume their rightful place on our tables.

Fortunately many of us recognize and appreciate the values of centuries long tradition, and at the same time are opting for organically produced ingredients, and almost-forgotten grains, when preparing traditional dishes.

The calorie content of the dishes in this book has been reduced without losing flavor. For example, in place of pork dripping, I use a minimal amount of vegetable oil. I would not wish to banish the smoked flavor so typical of much Hungarian cuisine, but I have reduced the quantity of smoked bacon to a quarter of the original amount, and found that the flavor of the dish is still the same. Of course some dishes are quite rich, but the calorie conscious reader can still enjoy savoring the idea behind the recipes without necessarily cooking them! However, remember that it's perfectly all right to share a lovely, hearty meal with friends and family once in a while without worrying about your waistline.

Allow yourself to enjoy the wonderful gutsy flavors of provincial cooking free of guilt, and remember our great grandmothers who had to make everything themselves, because pre-cooked ingredients, factory made pastas, jams, preserved fruits, tinned vegetables, or frozen filo pastry did not exist. I wish you a healthy appetite for these delicious dishes! *Egészségére!*

Júlia Frank

CONTENTS

HUNGARIAN PROVINCIAL COOKING
A BRIEF HISTORY

According to prehistoric sources and research, the daily nutrition of our ancestors was first defined by their foraging, fishing and hunting lifestyle. Later, horse-breeding, then the keeping of Hungarian grey cattle, *racka* sheep and chickens made a more varied way of eating possible. Meat, milk and dairy produce dominated nutrition. People used both sheep's and cow's milk to produce curd cheese, sour cream, butter and cheese, with buttermilk being a particular favorite.

Around 896 A.D., during the time of the Magyar conquest, Hungarians were allegedly the acknowledged experts in meat preservation. They cooked the butchered and skinned animal in a large iron kettle over an open fire, then boned, salted and smoked the meat. Once it was dried in the sun, the meat was ground into powder. This powder then only had to be thrown into boiling water for it to immediately swell up and re-constitute, providing a ready meal. Later, after the cultivation of plants had developed, grains and vegetables were mixed in with the meat powder. Thyme, tarragon, savory, lovage, basil and other green herbs grew wild in our homeland, while pungent and aromatic spices like black pepper, cinnamon, cloves, nutmeg, vanilla and ginger arrived in the Carpathian Basin – where modern Hungary is situated – after a long journey along the Chinese Silk route.

During military expeditions the Hungarian army was followed by herds of horses to secure food and milk for the soldiers, who won many battles by drawing their strength from eating fresh meat and the nutritious combination of the special dried vegetable-grain-meat powder. The armies of the expanding Hungarian nation regularly drank mare's milk and *koumiss*, a refreshingly tart, fermented milky drink with a slight alcohol content. Soldiers with a sweet tooth satisfied themselves by foraging for honey, or by tapping birch trees for sap. They also collected plenty of wild mushrooms and dried them, in order to supplement rations when on campaign. Good fishing was to be had in the richly populated lakes and rivers, and men also hunted in the woods in flood areas, or grazed their herds in meadows near water. Because both soldiers and hunters alike were often away from their families for weeks at a time, they needed food which did not spoil easily, such as grains and pasta, onions, bacon and vegetables.

The earliest vegetables grown in these times were onions, garlic, cabbage, carrots, marrow, sorrel, spinach, cucumber, beetroot, horseradish, peas, beans and lentils. Apples, pears, plums, peaches, cherries and grapes also provided a rich harvest from the loamy soil.

Most cooking was on the spit, or in kettles or clay pots over an open fire, resulting in the typically smoky flavor of many traditional Hungarian dishes.

Kettle goulash and mutton stew are still prepared in the same ancient way except, in our health-conscious times, we do not fry onions in bacon fat. Drawing on the rich offering of the rivers, at first Hungarian fish soup was made from a variety different fishes with onions and salt, with the hallmark use of paprika only appearing in the eighteenth century. Fish was also roasted on the spit or baked in clay. Since hunting was forbidden to the lower classes, hare, pheasant, venison or wild boar were rarely served in provincial dishes, and then usually only as a stew, where small cuts of meat could be used.

Bread has always been at the heart of Hungarian provincial cooking, although originally at the time of the Magyar conquest, the word 'bread' presumably referred to a yeast-free form of flat bread. The leavened bread and the sweet, plaited milk loaf called *kalács* which we know today appeared much later, with the dough made with yeast. For special occasions, bread dough was enlivened with dried fruit or finely chopped fresh pears, apples, or plums. Later still, the rich, slightly sweet dough of *kalács* was kneaded with milk and eggs and shaped into smaller rolls with a jam filling, or long rolls with a delicious walnut and poppy seed filling.

Bread was eaten with every kind of hot meal, as well as with bacon, meat, and dairy products. It was also commonly used as a thickening agent in cooking, or served as a porridge-like mush, or soaked with meat or vegetable juices.

The simplest form of everyday pasta was 'kneaded pastry', which consisted only of flour, salt and water. This was very widely used, being baked flat, then thinly rolled out or filled. With the addition of eggs, this basic pasta became *laska*, a type of irregular shaped pasta for garnishing soups. A popular provincial dish was the *táska* or 'bag' pasta, which was usually made from the simplest possible ingredients, and was only rarely prepared with the addition of eggs. The *táska* was made by thinly rolling the pastry while gently pulling it by hand, like a thicker version of filo pastry. This was then filled with fried onions, fresh curd cheese, or poppy seeds, and the resulting 10-15 cm. long 'bags' were cooked in boiling water. *Táska* could be eaten dipped in milk soup or served with onions in a black pepper and paprika flavored sauce.

The word *kása* refers to a soft, creamy puree of grains cooked in water, a type of dish as old as the cultivation of grains itself. Later, *kása* was also made from grains otherwise unsuitable for bread baking, such as millet and barley. These were joined by buckwheat in the fifteenth century, and corn in the seventeenth century. Rice had arrived from Asia earlier, during the opening of trade routes to the east at the beginning of the Magyar conquests.

These *kása* or grain mushes were indispensable in the everyday meals of common people. Sometimes they were cooked in the stock of beef, or goose giblets, and at other times simply in water or milk with butter. Hulled or coarsely ground barley, millet, buckwheat, corn, wheat or spelt were also used to make mushes, which would be eaten with milk, curd cheese, fried onions or cabbage, plum puree or browned breadcrumbs.

A delicious variation on *kása* was goose 'risotto', which was always prepared with millet cooked together with the goose and served with the meat. Another risotto-like dish was cooked with rice in beef or chicken stock.

Sterc was a simple dish made from flour dry roasted in a pan before adding a little water and fat. The mixture was then stirred until it formed coarse crumbles. Occasionally, the fat from pork or goose crackling was used to flavor the dish.

Puliszka, or cornmeal porridge, first appeared at the end of the seventeenth century. It also came in a Transylvanian variation called *bálmos*, the best-known kind being a cornmeal cooked in sheep's buttermilk.

Another type of *kása* was simply made with flour by slowly adding it to boiling liquid, and stirring the mixture continuously until it became very thick. The resulting paste was then spread out flat, cooled and cut into round shapes. This dish was called *gánica*, or sometimes *dödölle*. Folks in different regions added their own favorite toppings, such as sour cream and lard, fried onion or cabbage, browned breadcrumbs, milk, curd cheese or plum puree.

Csíramálé, or hoecake, a specialty made of sprouted grains, is one of the oldest sweets in Hungarian provincial cooking. A thin layer of rye, wheat or barley grains was spread out and kept moist until it sprouted. This was then ground into flour, with a little cornmeal added, and mixed with water. The mixture was then baked in a thin layer and provided a tasty finale to any meal.

Baked goods in medieval times included braided and round milk loaves, pies and *pogácsa* (a small, round, savory pastry still very much enjoyed in modern times). In the sixteenth century strudels and twists were introduced, and around 1600, pancakes similar to today's, but without filling. Provincial celebration sweets included pies, strudels, doughnuts, oven-baked milk loaves, the Transylvanian 'flue cake' and the ring cake. Typical everyday pastries were *pogácsa*, malt pastry, cornmeal cakes, curd cheese pie and pancakes.

Béles, or turnover-pie, was made with both sweet and savory fillings. The pastry was rolled out to a 3-4 millimeter thickness and the salted raw cabbage filling was folded into it. It was then placed on top of cabbage leaves, and baked at the bottom of a wood fired oven. Once baked the *béles* were kept in a cloth-covered basket so that the hard pastry would soften in the steam. At other times the *béles* were cut up into pieces, placed in a bowl, and softened with sour cream and fat. There are many kinds of *béles* fillings, including millet, cabbage, carrot, marrow, marrow-poppy seed, plain poppy seed, curd cheese, jam, apple and walnut.

Strudel was originally made without any filling, with just many layers of thin filo pastry. Filo pastry is made of flour, butter, milk, water and salt. A highly glutinous flour is necessary so that the pastry becomes extremely elastic, with thorough kneading being key to success. In Hungarian provincial cooking, many layers of filo pastry were smoothed into a baking tray, each brushed with melted butter. The pastry was then cut into smaller pieces, baked in a brick oven and served sprinkled with sugar. Later on, strudels were filled with a wide variety of produce, including creamed millet, rice or buckwheat, cabbage, carrots, marrow, poppy seed, curd cheese, jam, apples, plums, prunes, raisins, sour cherries, pumpkin seeds, walnuts, hazelnuts and beans.

Other traditional baked goods that can still be found on Hungarian tables today include:

kürtőskalács, or flue cake, which is made of a sweet yeasty dough that is rolled out thinly and cut into 2 cm. wide strips. These strips are wrapped around a wooden roller so that they overlap a little. As the roller is turned over charcoal embers, the cook keeps basting the cake with melted butter or duck fat, and glazing it with sugary egg white, and sometimes chopped walnuts.

The *golden ring doughnut* is a feather-light yeast dough fried in oil. *Twists* are also fried delicacies. They are smaller and crisper than doughnuts, and their dough is made with eggs and white wine.

In simple provincial households, pancakes meant a finger thick yeasty fare, whereas in contrast upper class kitchens often had pancakes made from a thin, yeast-free batter. The thick, yeasty pancakes were fried on both sides in a pan or on a hot stone, and were eaten sprinkled with sugar. The 'upper class' thin pancakes were filled with sweet curd cheese or plum puree and served folded in half.

Pogácsa, the simples of all pastries in provincial cooking, was prepared with fat and butter milk. Old Hungarian folk tales often talk about *pogácsa* baked in embers as fitting food for the hero's journey. In the nineteenth century, *pogácsa* with tiny pieces of crackling or pork fat were usually baked after a session of home butchering. Potato or curd cheese *pogácsa* was a more every day fare. *Pogácsa* kneaded with cooked potatoes (sometimes called *lepcsánka*) was baked on cabbage leaves in a traditional brick oven and was also eaten as a bread. *Tócsni* or *cicege* was a mixture of grated raw potatoes, buttermilk and finely chopped cracklings baked in the oven.

There were many variations of corn cakes which were very popular. *Prósza* consisted of corn meal, salt and buttermilk, and sometimes potatoes. Occasionally the cook might mix in marrow for a different flavor, and the *prósza* were always baked on an oven tray.

Cakes at the beginning of the nineteenth century were filled with jam, as well as preserved or fresh fruit. The innovation of sponge cakes with butter cream filling were only introduced later by the Budapest confectioner Henrik Kugler.

Herbs, Spices and Seasonings

Apart from the seasoning of dishes, a lot of salt was needed for the preservation of meat, bacon, fish, cabbage and pickles. The traditional herbs of Hungarian provincial cooking include savory, thyme, dill, marjoram, parsley, tarragon, celery, rosemary, sage, basil, caraway, vervain and saffron. These were either grown in the garden or picked wild. Armenians settling in Transylvania at the end of the seventeenth century introduced peppermint.

From the eighteenth century on, red paprika powder became the most Hungarian of all spices. It came to Hungary from the Balkans, and as far as we know, its cultivation began in the 1720s. In the Szeged and Kalocsa regions paprika had become so widespread that the emoluments of the village mayor and cantor included some paprika land, and workers were given paprika as an allowance in kind. The first goulash, called 'paprika meat', was cooked in 1786 in Szeged, but at first paprika was used by common people only as a replacement for expensive imported black pepper. (At this time all varieties of paprika were hot.) Paprika played a vital role in goulash becoming a national dish. By the Reform Era in the 1800s, paprika chicken had also become a typical Hungarian dish.

Sugar was considered a spice and was used sparingly, because imported cane sugar was very expensive. As an interesting aside, it took four hundred years for sugar to be used in cooking at all, since a tenth-century tradition relegated it to the field of medicine.

The career of bouillon, as well as *gulyás*, pörkölt and *paprikás,* all of the goulash family, started slowly but continues in full force today. Dishes with meat and sauerkraut have become standard fare on festive and wedding menus. Stuffed cabbage, for example, became standard fare on tables throughout the country, while in the Great Plain region, pörkölt and *paprikás* pushed out every other dish from special, festive menus. Beef and chicken soups were also very popular. Vegetables and small pasta were cooked together with the meat, and people ate the meat that had been cooked in the broth with horseradish or other sauces.

Vegetables

Peas and lentils were already cultivated in Hungary in the Middle Ages. There was only one hard skinned variety of bean known as the 'horse bean' that was not popular. The forerunners of today's beans probably originated in America.

In the Middle Ages, cabbage patches were a regular feature of Hungarian villages, and cabbage pickling was widely popular all around the country. Turnip was also grown in gardens, and some of it was pickled in a similar way to cabbage.

Of the gourd family, only bottle gourd originated in Europe, with all other varieties coming from America. In the eighteenth century pumpkin was cultivated all around the country, while on the other hand the consumption of marrow became popular in the provinces only in the twentieth century, when urban tastes made their way to the countryside.

Green pepper, tomato and potato plants also originated in America. At first the tomato was merely an ornamental plant enjoyed by upper class gardeners, and only later did it become considered a food. Farmers all around Hungary started growing tomatoes from around the beginning of the nineteenth century. The earliest method of preserving tomatoes was by drying: they were pushed through a coarse sieve, dried crisp in an earthenware dish in the oven, and then stored in crushed form in linen bags.

Potatoes became the most important of the new vegetables, as they were highly suitable for feeding the poor and common people, especially in times of grain scarcity.

Sorrel and mushrooms remained vegetables which could be gathered in the wild, their only cost being the time spent finding them.

Hungarian provincial cooking developed many dishes made of beans and lentils, most of which were purées and mushes. If there was no proper cut of meat to accompany the pulses these were eaten topped with fried onions or fatty bacon.

Pumpkin was regularly used a long while before marrow came into the picture. Because of its many seeds it was believed to bring good fortune, because the seeds were considered to symbolize coins. For the same reason, other 'good luck' ingredients included grain dishes, peas, lentils or beans. Potatoes were not only creamed, casseroled and cooked as a soup, but also used for sauces, garnishes and soufflés. Until the twentieth century potatoes were not considered to be a garnish for meat in provincial cooking, but rather were used creamed, in soups, or for mushes. Potatoes with onions was eaten as a main dish in almost the entire Hungarian speaking region. In Transdanubia and in the North-East, the dish was made from boiled potatoes that had been previously cooked, peeled and chopped. In other regions the potatoes would be boiled whole in their skin, or sometimes baked. Whatever the regional variation, once cooked, the potatoes would then be mashed and fried with onions.

Another popular and simple potato dish was a puree made from mashed potatoes mixed with flour. This was either served as a mush or cut into bite sized pieces. If cooked as a mush, the puree would most often be served topped with fried onion and fat. On the other hand, bite sized pieces enjoyed more diverse toppings such as poppy seed, curd cheese, sour cream and fat, fried onions, cabbage, or browned breadcrumbs. Some exotic sounding names for these potato dishes include *zsámiska, dödölle, gánica,* and *ganca.*

Many a winter breakfast consisted of potatoes boiled or baked whole. Lunch was often some creamed vegetable, with or without meat.

Soup

In modern times soup was the only kind of food served every day. Most often it was thickened with the addition of bread or eggs. Thickening with a *roux,* made by frying flour in fat, was a method described in contemporary cookery books but rarely used in practice.

Countless variations of soups developed in provincial cooking with meat soups and bouillons leading the way. Clear broths made from fresh beef or chicken with parsley root, carrots, and a whole onion, were often served for Sunday lunch or special occasions. Such broths were also the most popular soups at wedding meals. They were not soured, however *Csorba,* a Romanian meat soup served in Transylvanian restaurants, was a similar clear broth, but soured with the addition of vinegar.

Other piquant soups like *kaszásleves* (mower's soup) were made with smoked meat and soured with a little vinegar. Its many variations include 'pale' or 'red', the latter made with paprika, but both thickened with sour cream, eggs, or *roux*. In some places cooked meat was eaten together with the soup, while elsewhere meat was eaten after the soup course. In the nineteenth century, in parts of the Palóc region, a piquant meat soup made with mutton offal thickened with milk and soured with vinegar was the only soup on wedding menus. Bean, lentil and potato soups were all enriched with smoked meat. An old variety of soup, more like a casserole dish, consisted of beans, prunes and smoked meat thickened with sour cream. Two other famous piquant soups flavored with vinegar were made with lungs and tripe. At home butchering time, the liquid resulting from the cooking of stuffing meat and the boiling of liver and blood sausages was also consumed as a soup.

Goulash soup evolved from goulash stew and became notable from around 1880, while the most popular vegetable soup was green bean soup.

Thick lentil and bean soups were regularly served on fast days, when meat was prohibited. Beans were also cooked in milk or in plenty of water, with most of the softened beans then being strained. The cooking liquid was eaten as a soup, and the beans eaten as a mush. In mushroom growing regions people added mushroom to the bean mush, and later quinces were combined with beans for more variety.

A soup made with the pickling liquid of sauerkraut was thickened with flour, or garnished with mush or pasta. Both pickled and fresh cabbage soups contained some meat, or sometimes, mushroom. Mushroom soup was made using both dried and fresh mushrooms. In regions where they pickled turnip, recipes were developed for soups using both pickled and fresh turnip.

The many variations of potato soups were widely popular. The cooking liquid of beans, lentils, potatoes or pasta was often seasoned and spiced to ascend through the ranks and become promoted to a soup. Vegetable soup was also cooked with these liquids with the addition of carrots and parsley, but tomato soup was a twentieth century addition to provincial cooking.

Pasta was cooked for many of the above mentioned soups as a garnish, but there were also numerous thick and clear soups featuring meat or milk broth, or pasta. East of the Danube, in the Great Hungarian Plain region, the pasta pellets were browned in bacon fat. Soup garnishes included vermicelli, small square shaped or grated pasta, stuffed pasta pouches, and wheat, buckwheat or corn dumplings.

Milk soups were made with full milk or with a mixture of milk and water garnished with grain mush, pasta, dumplings, beans or potatoes.

'Soup on bread' was the name given to curd cheese or cheese soup. Curd cheese soup was made by boiling sweetened milk, thickening it with sour cream and serving it with the curd cheese. Cheese soup was a specialty made from warm buttermilk curd cheese.

Until the turn of the nineteenth century *keszőce* or *cibere,* a soup made of the fermented liquid of wheat bran was very popular in the whole Hungarian speaking area. Later fresh fruit soups 'inherited' these names. Fruit *cibere* was made from both fresh and dried fruit and thickened with sour cream.

One of the simplest soups ever was caraway soup: water and roasted caraway seeds were added to a *roux* and the soup was seasoned and garnished with pasta or eggs.

Thickening with bacon fat and *roux* were the most frequently used methods, but sometimes melted dripping was used to flavor the soup, or else fried onions and paprika, or sour cream, milk or buttermilk.

Milk and Dairy Products

Milk and dairy products, together with eggs, used to be typical foods on fast days.

Fresh or dried curd cheese, butter and yoghurt were the most traditional dairy products in medieval Hungary. *Vaj* (butter) is a Finno-Ugric word, *túró* (curd cheese) and *sajt* (cheese) are borrowed from the Ancient Turkish. Modern cheese made with rennet was brought to Hungary by Alpine cheese makers in the seventeenth century.

Hungarian common people hardly ate any proper cheese. Alpine cheese makers were called in and employed as tenant farmers to produce cheese on the estates of the landed gentry.

The most common curd cheese dish was made from either fresh or dried curd cheese combined with milk or sour cream, eggs and dill. This mixture was boiled with a little water and served on slices of bread. A more simple variation consisted of mixed fresh curd cheese with sour cream, butter, onions and salt heated together in a pan. This was also served poured over slices of bread or as a topping for pasta.

As an alternative to soup, a bowl of fresh milk with pieces of bread in it was often taken for winter breakfasts. After 1830 boiled or baked potatoes were eaten for breakfast with milk, and milk was also added to grain mushes. Standard summer breakfasts of bread and bacon were often eaten outdoors in the fields. Curd cheese or cheese replaced this traditional fare only on fast days. During seasons of mowing, harvesting, gathering and threshing the farmer and his workers regularly ate buttermilk, for its cooling properties. Festive menus always included grain meals cooked in milk, as well as curd cheese pie.

Eggs were eaten fried or breaded as a main meal. *Kukó*, a provincial egg dish was cooked in empty egg shells. The filling was either millet with pieces of lung or corn mush with smoked meat added. The filled egg shells were cooked in boiling water and served in the seasoned liquid. Sometimes thick almond milk, colored with saffron or spicy scrambled eggs was used as a filling.

Bacon

Before the introduction of cooking fat, a whole host of dishes were prepared with bacon. The bacon pieces were either added to the other ingredients at the beginning and cooked together, or a small piece of bacon was first fried and its fat used in the dish. Bacon was very highly esteemed. Sauerkraut with meat, one of the most popular dishes of the early modern era, would never be complete without a piece of bacon cooked in it.

Pickles

A big tub of cabbage was pickled in every household. In some places whole cabbages were put into the tub and enough salty water to cover them was poured in. The whole cabbage heads were then cut up when they were used in dishes. In other places the tub was filled with sliced cabbages, with only the occasional whole head in between intended for wrapping the famous 'stuffed cabbage', or *töltött káposzta*. Each layer of sliced cabbage was salted and compressed by treading, or by the application of weights such as stones. Water was not poured on in this version, but fragrant local herbs with properties to aid preservation were added. Turnips were also pickled by being sliced, salted and compressed in a tub without water.

A great variety of cabbage dishes were prepared, mostly from sauerkraut and fresh cabbage when the supply of pickled cabbage ran out. These variations included: stuffed cabbage, cabbage in tomato sauce, stir-fried cabbage, and sauerkraut cooked with millet or pearl barley. Barley was used in meaty sauerkraut dishes as well. 'Heyduck' cabbage was made from finely chopped fresh cabbage braised in vinegar, garlic and fat. Sauerkraut with beans was an unusual combination. (In certain regions the same dish was called sauerkraut with peas because beans were called peas!) The beans were cooked separately and added to the sauerkraut that had been cooked in water. If smoked meat was to be included it had to be cooked together with the cabbage. These dishes were then thickened with a *roux* or with a flour-water paste. Meaty and beanie cabbage dishes were typical winter food, and before beans were introduced, sauerkraut had often been combined with peas in Hungarian provincial kitchens.

Salads

Salads were not eaten as a starter or as a main course. In the spring wild lettuce was picked in the meadows, where the delicious leaves began to grown in loose soil under the snow cover. Lettuce also came in a garden variety and both types were used for making fresh salads dressed with vinegar and oil, or bacon fat. In Transdanubia and in the Great Hungarian Plain, lettuce leaves were withered and had a hot dressing poured over them. Exactly when fresh cucumber salad began to be used is uncertain, but it became a regular companion to the dry flour *sterc,* a dish previously eaten with milk or buttermilk. Buttermilk was also used as a dressing for cucumber salad. In some places salads were made from onions and radishes, served with a simple vinaigrette. Slices of pickled onion rings were also popular as a winter or fast day dish. Pickled beetroot and leavened gherkins were also regularly prepared at home.

In the nineteenth century pickling peppers was already widespread in pepper growing areas. *Marc* was put at the bottom of a barrel or tub, followed by a layer of peppers, then marc again, alternating the two ingredients until the barrel was full. Slightly salted water was then poured in. Later, vinegar was substituted for marc, and pickled miniature watermelons and green tomatoes were added.

Vegetables like sauerkraut or pickled carrots preserved for winter were also used as salads, often sprinkled with oil or hot bacon fat. An early form of pepper pickling was to put a few layers of hot peppers in between layers of cabbage.

At old provincial wedding festivities the boiled meat from the soup was eaten with sauces. At wealthier wedding celebrations – we only know menus from the eighteenth century onwards – the meat was a roast. This was the place for salads, in most cases winter pickles, since most weddings were held in winter. From the mid-nineteenth century in the Great

Plain area, goulash gradually became an important part of wedding meals. This created a new opportunity for serving pickled vegetables. In the twentieth century the usual pickles on a wedding menu were gherkins, beetroot and peppers.

In the area between the Danube and the Tisza rivers, pickled peppers were a regular part of summer breakfasts, usually eaten with bacon and boiled potatoes or bread. In the weeks following pig slaughtering pickles were often served to accompany the rich, fatty dishes, and were also eaten throughout the year with goulash. During fasting seasons fresh lettuce and onion salad were eaten on their own with bread, and the same held true for sauerkraut in winter. For summer meals in the fields, instead of pickles, the picnic basket would include raw onions, raw cucumber, radish, and hot and sweet peppers.

In more modern times provincial kitchen sauces were either eaten with boiled or smoked meat or as an independent dish, and from the end of the eighteenth century horseradish sauce was the most popular, later followed by tomato sauce, then onion and garlic sauce. These were old fashioned white sauces without paprika, usually served with smoked meat. Nettle, sorrel, cucumber, rhubarb and mushroom sauces were all popular. Fruit sauces were mainly prepared from tart fruits like cooking apples, dogberries and later sour cherries. Another simple, sauce-like dish was prepared from prunes thickened with sour cream. In West Transdanubia, white sauces with a base of flour and milk or sour cream and fragrant green herbs were made with rosemary, while in Transylvania, tarragon was the main herb, replaced by parsley in other regions. Later paprika powder was added to onion sauce to be served with boiled meat.

COUNTRY: BREAKFAST
POTATO PRÓSZA ▶▶

CONTEMPORARY RECIPES FOR TRADITIONAL DISHES

The recipes serve four unless otherwise stated.

SOUPS

Chicken soup

(for 8-10)

1 large chicken (3-4 lbs / 1.5-2 kg), depending on the weight of the chicken,
1.5-2 lbs / 750 g-1 kg mixed stock vegetables (carrots, parsley roots, kohlrabi, celeriac,
green bell pepper), 1 large onion, 3 oz / 100 g fresh mushrooms (or 1 tbsp dried),
1 small cauliflower, 1 slice savoy cabbage, 1 small bunch green beans,
2 tbsp shelled green peas, 1 tomato, 1 bunch each parsley and celery tops,
3 cloves garlic, 10 whole black peppercorns, 1 bay leaf, 1 small piece lovage root
or 1 bunch lovage greens, a small piece of mace, 3 crushed cardamom pods,
2 cloves, pinch sugar, 1 heaped tbsp salt
For garnish: *2 oz / 50 g vermicelli or small shell pasta*

Preparation: Cut the chicken into portions, remove any excess fat and add to a large, deep pot. Add the herbs in an infuser and the washed, unpeeled onion and peeled garlic cloves cut in half. Cover with 6-7 pints / 3 liters of cold water and place on stove.

Cooking: Bring the water to a boil uncovered, over a medium heat. Turn the heat down to the lowest setting and gently simmer for 2 hours without stirring. Meanwhile peel the root vegetables and leave them whole. Add all the vegetables to the pot except the celery tops, parsley and fresh lovage greens. Cook until all the vegetables are tender. Turn off the heat and let it rest for 30 minutes. Strain the soup through a very fine sieve gently ladling the liquid. Discard the onion and serve the chicken and the vegetables on separate plates. Finely chop the green herbs, sprinkle them over the clear stock, and serve with the pasta that had been cooked separately. Serve the chicken and the vegetables as a second course with horseradish or tomato sauce.

Note: Parsley root is the root of flat leaf parsley and it is widely used for stock making in Hungary. Although its flavor is a little different, it can be substituted with parsnip. 'Mixed stock vegetables' always mean carrots, parsley root, 1 kohlrabi and 1 small celeriac bulb. Add all the vegetables to the soup slowly, making sure it does not stop simmering.

Beef broth

(for 8)

*2.5 lbs / 1 kg beef (brisket or bony neck), 2.5 lbs / 1 kg bones
(also marrowbone, if available), vegetables and spices listed
above for chicken soup*

Preparation: Throw the bones into boiling water, let it boil again and strain. Tie a string around the marrowbones to prevent the marrow oozing out during cooking. Pour the strained liquid back into the pot. Add the meat and serve.

Cooking: After 2.5-3 hours of simmering, add the whole pieces of peeled vegetables and cook until tender. After 30 minutes strain the soup. Serve the meat and vegetables on separate plates. Cut off the strings from the marrowbones, and hit the bones at one end so the soft marrow slides out. Spread it on hot slices of toast, and serve sprinkled with paprika, black pepper and salt.

Note: 'Paprika' means dried, red paprika powder in all the recipes.

Lamb soup

(for 6)

*2.5 lbs / 1kg lamb offal (or bony parts of lamb), 1 large onion,
1 cup sour cream, 1 bunch fresh dill, 2 tbsp oil, 1 level tbsp flour,
1 tsp paprika, 3 cloves garlic, salt to taste, ground black pepper,
1 tbsp mild vinegar*

Preparation: Wash, dice and pat dry the lamb. Sauté the peeled and finely chopped onion in oil, remove from the heat for a minute while adding the paprika. Pour in 2 tbsp of water, put it back to the stove and add the diced lamb. Brown the lamb pieces stirring constantly, add the salt, and 4 pints / 2 liters of water.

Cooking: Add the peeled and crushed garlic and the black pepper. Cook until the meat becomes tender. Mix the flour with 1 tbsp of vinegar (tarragon or apple cider) and sour cream, and add this mixture to the boiling soup. Cook for a few more minutes and serve sprinkled with chopped fresh dill.

Green bean soup
with smoked knuckle of ham
(for 6)

1 small smoked knuckle of ham, 1 lb 2 oz / 500 g fresh green beans,
1 cup sour cream, 2 tomatoes, 1 large onion, 2 tbsp oil,
1 large bunch each parsley and dill (dried dill can be substituted)
2 cloves garlic, 1 tsp paprika, salt

Preparation: Soak the smoked ham in cold water overnight. Next day pour fresh water over it and cook until the meat falls off the bone. Chop it into small pieces and set it aside. Boil some water, add the tomatoes and leave them to soak for 2 minutes. Drain and peel off the skins. Sauté the finely chopped onion in oil until golden. Remove from the heat and mix in the paprika. Add the sautéed onion to the cooking liquid of the ham.

Cooking: Add the cleaned green beans cut into 1 inch / 2-3 cm pieces, and cook until tender. Add the smoked ham pieces, throw in the finely chopped parsley and dill, and the peeled and slices tomatoes. Flavor with crushed garlic. Add enough water to make up to about 3 pints / 1.5 liters. Boil together thoroughly and pour in the sour cream. Turn off the heat and let it stand covered for five minutes.

Note: Tinned green beans do not need cooking, only heating. Frozen beans need half the cooking time of fresh ones. Please note that in recipes where you add paprika powder to roux you always remove the dish from the heat for a minute because paprika can turn bitter if overheated.

Hungarian tripe soup

1 lb 2 oz / 500 g beef tripe, 1 cup sour cream, 1 large onion,
1 green bell pepper, 1 tomato, 3 tbsp oil, 1 tsp dried marjoram, 1 tsp flour,
1 bay leaf, half tsp each ground black pepper and grated lemon rind,
1 pinch sugar, salt and vinegar to taste

Preparation: Cut the carefully cleaned tripe into strips, and pour a mixture of hot water and vinegar over it. Drain, and cook the tripe in plenty of fresh salted water. Drain again.

Cooking: Gently sauté the peeled and finely chopped onion in oil. Fry tripe strips, taking it off the heat just for a minute to mix in the paprika. Pour in 2 pints / 1 liter of water. Add sliced green pepper, peeled and sliced tomatoes, bay leaf, herbs, seasoning and lemon rind, and cook for ten minutes. Mix the flour with the sour cream and add to boiling soup stirring continuously. Let it boil for a few minutes and add a pinch of sugar and a little vinegar. Serve hot.

Potato soup
with sauerkraut and sausage

1 lb 2 oz / 500 g potatoes, 8 oz / 250 g sauerkraut, 8 oz / 250 g soft smoked sausage,
1 cup sour cream, 2 oz / 50 g smoked bacon, 1 small onion, 1 tbsp each flour and salt,
half tsp each dried savory and ground black pepper, 1 tsp paprika,
1 small hot chili, 1 pinch sugar

Preparation: Peel and dice the potatoes, and chop the sauerkraut. Chop the peeled onion and the bacon. Wash the smoked sausage, peel off the skin and slice. Fry the bacon pieces until the fat runs, stirring all the time. Remove the crisp pieces from the fat and set aside.

Cooking: Lightly fry the flour in the bacon fat until pale golden. Take it off the heat to add paprika and onion. Pour in 1.5 cups / 300 ml cold water and let it boil, stirring continuously. When the onion-paprika *roux* becomes smooth in texture add another 18 fl oz / half liter water, and the potato pieces. Season with salt and pepper, add savory and hot pepper and cook over a very low heat. When the potatoes are cooked add sauerkraut and sausage slices. Once sauerkraut is cooked add sugar and more salt to taste and add sour cream mixed with half cup / 100 ml of water. Let it boil for a few minutes and serve sprinkled with crisp bacon pieces. This soup is best eaten the day after cooking because its flavor will have had time to mature fully.

Note: If the potatoes are cooked together with the sauerkraut they will not become soft because the acid from the sauerkraut hardens them.

Piquant lentil soup

8 oz / 250 g mixed stock vegetables, 8 oz / 250 g potatoes,
7 oz / 200 g lentils, 1 cup sour cream, 2 oz / 50 g smoked bacon, 1 leek,
1 medium onion, 2 celery tops, 1 tbsp flour, 1 bay leaf, 2 cloves garlic,
3 cloves, mild vinegar or lemon juice to taste, ground black pepper, salt

Preparation: Soak the lentils overnight. Cut the potatoes into small cubes. Finely chop the onion, celery tops, vegetables and leek. Cut the bacon into small pieces and fry until crisp. Throw all the vegetables – except the potatoes – in with the bacon, and fry over a high heat for two minutes.

Cooking: Add the drained lentils to the vegetables, add bay leaf, garlic, cloves, salt and pepper and pour in 1.5 pints / 700 ml water. Cook slowly, covered with a lid. After about 45 minutes add the potatoes. When they are soft, pour in the sour cream and flour mixture and boil for a few minutes. Season well and add a little vinegar or lemon juice to taste.

Bean soup with tarragon

8 oz / 250 g mixed stock vegetables, 7 oz / 200 g large variety beans,
1 cup sour cream, 1 bunch fresh or 1 tsp dried tarragon, 2 tbsp oil,
1 level tbsp flour, 1 clove garlic, 1 tsp paprika, salt and a pinch of sugar to taste,
tarragon or other vinegar

Preparation: Soak the beans overnight in cold water. Drain and cook in 2 pints / 1 liter of fresh water until almost completely tender. (You can cut cooking time to one quarter by using a pressure cooker!) Peel vegetables and cut them into batons.

Cooking: Add the prepared vegetables to the beans and cook until tender. Make a pale golden *roux* from the oil and the flour, remove from the heat for a minute to add the paprika, half the finely chopped tarragon, and crushed garlic. Dilute with 3.5 fl oz / 100 ml of cold water, stirring continuously. Add this mixture to the soup together with the sour cream, salt, vinegar, a pinch of sugar and the remaining tarragon. Boil everything together for 5-10 minutes and serve hot.

Sauerkraut soup with wild mushrooms

14 oz / 400 g sauerkraut, 8 oz / 250 g wild mushrooms
(porcini, chanterelle or any other selection), 1 cup sour cream,
1 onion, 2 oz / 50 g smoked bacon, 1 tbsp flour, 1 tbsp dried savory,
salt to taste

Preparation: Peel and finely chop the onion. Wash the mushrooms thoroughly under running water, pat dry and slice. Chop the sauerkraut and fry finely chopped bacon.
Cooking: Fry the chopped onion in bacon fat, add mushrooms. Season with salt, cover and steam until soft. Add sauerkraut, savory, fry for 2 minutes and pour in 1.5 pints / 1 liter of water. Cook until tender. Mix the flour with 2 fl oz / 50 ml of water and sour cream and add to soup. Let it boil for a few minutes stirring all the time.
Note: Fresh mushrooms must not be soaked because their precious protein leaches out. Dried mushrooms can be soaked overnight in just enough water to cover them. The mushrooms will soak up the water by next morning and can be used as fresh.

Bean soup with prunes

8 oz / 250 g dried cannellini beans, 8 oz / 250 g prunes,
8 oz / 250 g smoked meat, 1 cup sour cream, 1 large onion, 1 bunch fresh tarragon,
3 cloves garlic, salt and pepper to taste

Preparation: Soak the beans, prunes and smoked meat in three separate bowls overnight. Next day, stone the prunes and save their soaking liquid. Peel and finely chop the onion and the tarragon. Drain both the beans and meat. Cut the smoked meat into small cubes or slices.
Cooking: Place the beans and the smoked meat into a large pot. Sprinkle it with chopped onion and pepper, pour in the soaking liquid from the prunes and add enough water to make it up to 2 pints / 1.2 liters. Cover and cook until almost done, then add the prunes. Finally add crushed garlic, chopped tarragon and sour cream.

Lebbencs soup

(for 6)

1 lb / 500 g potatoes, 8 oz / 250 g mixed stock vegetables, 4 oz / 100 g egg pasta squares,
1 cup sour cream, 4 oz / 100 g smoked bacon, 1 large onion, 1 large bunch parsley,
1 tbsp paprika, 2 cloves garlic, 1 heaped tsp salt, 1 tsp flour, half tsp ground black pepper

Preparation: Peel, wash and cut the potatoes into small cubes. Peel and slice the stock vegetables. Finely chop the smoked bacon and fry it until crisp. Leave half the bacon fat in the pan and hold the other half in reserve.

Cooking: Sauté the finely chopped onion in half the fat, remove from the heat to mix in the paprika and immediately add two tablespoons of water. Return to the heat, add the potato cubes and the vegetables. Season with salt and pepper and pour in 4 pints / 2 liters of water. Cover and cook until almost tender. Brown the dry pasta squares in the remaining bacon fat, add to the potatoes and cook until they are both done. Finally, thicken with sour cream mixed with crushed garlic and flour, let it boil for five minutes and sprinkle with chopped fresh parsley.

Note: *Lebbencs* is a wafer thin dried egg pasta with irregular shapes. Although lasagna sheets are much thicker, you can try to break them up into smaller pieces to use them for this recipe.

Caraway soup

2 oz / 50 g flour, 3 tbsp oil, 1 egg, 1 level tbsp salt, 1 tsp caraway seeds,
1 tsp paprika

Preparation: Gently heat the oil, sprinkle in the flour and carefully brown it while stirring continuously. Mix in the caraway seeds, remove from the heat and let them all pop. Add the paprika, pour in 12 fl oz / 300 ml of cold water and mix until smooth.

Cooking: Add another 1 pint / 500 ml of water to the *roux,* and let it boil again. Add salt and keep stirring. Finally beat the egg until frothy and pour it into the boiling soup in a steady stream.

Note: Caraway soup is usually served with croutons.

CATFISH STEW

DAIRY AND EGG DISHES

Provincial breakfast

6 eggs, 4 oz / 100 g smoked bacon, 2 medium sized potatoes, 2 green bell peppers,
1 large onion, salt, black pepper and paprika to taste

Preparation: Beat the eggs until frothy, add salt and pepper. Peel and thinly slice the potatoes, peel and finely chop the onion. Slice the green peppers, cut the bacon into small cubes. Fry the bacon pieces in a large non-stick frying pan.
Cooking: Brown the potato slices on both sides in bacon fat, add the chopped onion and the green pepper slices. Fry until everything is cooked through, add the beaten eggs. Arrange the potato slices, chopped onion and green pepper pieces evenly in the egg. Fry until the bottom layer is cooked. If there are raw patches on top tilt the frying pan and let the runny part slide to the edges. Use a fork to help ease the cooked parts. Cut into four wedges and serve sprinkled with paprika or black pepper.

Domika

1 lb / 400 g day-old bread, 2 cups sour cream, 7 oz / 200 g grated cheese,
7 fl oz / 200 ml milk, 3 eggs, 2 bunches parsley, salt to taste, ground black pepper,
2 oz / 50 g butter; 2 tbsp oil for the oven proof baking dish, 2 tbsp bread crumbs.

Preparation: Slice the bread thinly. Beat the eggs and mix with the milk and sour cream. Season and add finely chopped parsley. Melt the butter.
Cooking: Oil a medium sized baking dish and coat it thinly with breadcrumbs. Put half the bread slices at the bottom. Sprinkle with half the cheese and pour half the egg mixture over. Repeat the bread, cheese and egg mixture layers. Pour melted butter evenly on top and cover tightly with foil. Bake covered in a preheated hot oven for 20 minutes. Take off the foil cover and bake until golden brown. Cut into squares and serve with more sour cream on top.
Note: Left-over bread or rolls can be used up for this recipe. You can use yoghurt or cream instead of sour cream or a mixture of all three.

'Smoked' curd cheese

8 oz / 250 g sheep's curd cheese, 4 oz / 100 g smoked bacon, half cup sour cream,
1 small onion, 2 bunches fresh chives, salt and black pepper to taste

Preparation: Chop the smoked bacon into very fine pieces. Fry until crisp, and drain the fat. Chop the chives.

Cooking: Mix the curd cheese with the crisp bacon pieces, 1 tbsp of fat, sour cream and grated or very finely chopped onion. Season well, add the chopped chives. Thoroughly beat the mixture together, pile it into a cone shape on a glass platter and refrigerate. Serve with slices of crusty bread.

Note: Sheep's curd cheese is a very typical Hungarian ingredient with a pungent, salty flavor. Crumbled sheep's feta cheese can be a good substitute.

Rice pudding with plum purée

7 oz / 200 g pudding rice, 1.5 pints / 800 ml milk, 1.5 oz / 40 g butter,
2-3 tbsp sugar, half tsp salt; plum purée for topping

Preparation: Wash the rice in a colander and let it drip.

Cooking: Melt the butter in a non-stick frying pan, add the rice and turn around gently for a couple of minutes until all the grains are coated with butter. Add 8 fl oz / 200 ml water and half the milk. Add salt, and cook over a very low heat until the rice absorbs all the liquid. Add the remaining milk and cook until the pudding becomes creamy in texture. Keep stirring to break up the rice grains. It is ready when soft and moist. Mix in the sugar, portion it on plates and serve topped with plum purée.

Note: Plum purée or plum jam is a specialty of Hungary. Plums are cooked in cauldrons for many hours (sometimes a whole day) without any added sugar, until they turn into a rich, dark, thick purée.

CREAMED VEGETABLES
AND OTHER VEGETABLE DISHES

(Creamed vegetables are often eaten in Hungary as a main course,
accompanied by meat, eggs or sausages.)

Vegetable dish of beans

11 oz / 300 g dried mottled beans, 2 large onions, 1 cup sour cream,
2 tbsp oil, 1 heaped tbsp flour, 1 level tsp salt

Preparation: Wash the beans and soak them overnight. Next day discard the soaking water and cook the beans in just enough fresh water to cover them. Finely chop the onions.
Cooking: Fry the flour in oil to a pale golden color, mix in the onions and cook for another minute. Pour in the cooking liquid from the beans and cook until it thickens, stirring continuously. Season with salt, mix in three quarters of the sour cream and the cooked beans, let it boil for a few minutes. Finally top it with the remaining sour cream and serve with fried *wiener wurst* or other sausages.

Vegetable dish of yellow split peas

8 oz / 250 g yellow peas, 1 medium carrot, 1 onion,
1 tomato (or half tsp tomato purée), 2 tbsp oil, 1 tbsp flour, 1 clove garlic,
salt, pepper, oregano, basil and thyme

Preparation: Soak the yellow peas overnight. Next day sauté the chopped onions and sliced carrots in oil.
Cooking: Pour in 2 pints / 1 liter water, add crushed garlic, drained yellow peas, peeled tomato and salt. Season with pepper, oregano, basil and thyme. Let the mixture boil and cook covered until soft. Mix the flour with 1 cup of cooking liquid, add this mixture to the yellow pea mixture and cook together for a few minutes. Serve with fried sausages.

[27]

Creamed lentils

8 oz / 250 g lentils, 1 cup sour cream,
1 cup cooking liquid from smoked meat, 1 small onion,
2 tbsp oil, 1 tbsp flour, salt and sugar to taste

Preparation: Carefully sift through the lentils and discard any unsuitable ones and small stones. Wash, drain and cook the sifted lentils in salted water until tender.
Cooking: Heat the oil, add the flour, let it brown gently and mix in the finely chopped onion. Dilute this *roux* with the smoked meat cooking liquid, keep stirring and let it boil. Use this mixture to thicken the lentils. Flavor with a pinch of sugar, sour cream and cook for another five minutes.
Note: Lentils should not be cooked in a pressure cooker because they can block the safety valve!

Sauerkraut with beans

1 lb / 500 g sauerkraut, 7 oz / 200 g dried beans,
1 pint / 500 ml cooking liquid from smoked meat (or the same amount
of water with a stock cube), 1 large onion, 1 cup sour cream, 2 tbsp oil,
1 tsp paprika, ground black pepper

Preparation: Soak the sorted and washed beans overnight in cold water. Next day drain and cook beans in flavored cooking liquid until tender.
Cooking: While the beans are cooking, sauté the finely chopped onion in oil, then remove from the heat to add paprika and 2 tbsp water. Add the chopped sauerkraut and cook covered, stirring often. Add sauerkraut to the cooked beans. Season with black pepper, mix in sour cream and let it boil for five minutes.

Cabbage in tomato sauce

2 lbs / 1 kg white cabbage, 1 pint / half liter tomato juice
(or 1 small tin of tomato purée mixed with 2 cups / 450 ml water),
2 tbsp flour, 2 tbsp oil, 1 small onion, salt and sugar to taste

Preparation: Wash and thinly slice the cabbage. Put it in just enough salted water to cover, together with the finely chopped onion, and cook until tender.

Cooking: Sauté the flour in oil to a golden color, add the tomato juice and let it boil while stirring all the time. (If it becomes lumpy, push it through a fine sieve.) Add this thick *roux* to the cooked cabbage, season with salt and sugar and let it boil for 6-7 minutes.

Creamed marrow

3 lbs / 1.5 kg marrow, 12 fl oz / 300 ml buttermilk, 1 small onion,
1 bunch fresh dill, 2 tbsp oil, 1 tbsp flour, 1 level tsp paprika, 1 tsp vinegar,
pinch of sugar, salt to taste

Preparation: Peel and shred the marrow. (For this you may need a special gadget to produce long, thin threads of marrow. In the absence of this use the coarse blade of a grater.) Salt it well, let it stand for 15 minutes and then gently squeeze out the excess liquid. Sauté the flour in oil until pale golden, add the finely chopped onion, and remove from the heat to add the paprika. Mix well, pour in half cup / 100 ml of water and buttermilk, let it boil.

Cooking: Add the marrow threads to the *roux* together with the buttermilk, add a little vinegar, mix and cook for 15 minutes. Keep stirring to prevent burning. Finally add finely chopped dill, let it boil for a minute and add a little sugar.

Note: Cream marrow is often served with fried eggs.

Creamed sorrel with eggs

1.5 lb / 750 g fresh sorrel leaves, 1 cup / 200 ml milk, half cup / 50 ml cream,
1 egg, 2 tbsp oil, 1 tbsp flour, sugar, salt

Preparation: Put the washed and drained sorrel leaves through a mincer (or chop very finely), cover and sauté in hot oil for a few minutes. Beat the egg.

Cooking: Sprinkle the wilted sorrel with flour, fry for 2-3 minutes, pour in the milk, cream and half cup of water. Let it boil while stirring all the time. Add salt, sugar and the beaten egg. Let it boil for 2 minutes until it thickens.

Piquant creamed potatoes with bay leaf

2 lbs / 1 kg potatoes, 1 cup sour cream, 1 small onion,
2 tbsp oil, 2 tbsp flour, 2 bay leaves, vinegar, salt and sugar to taste

Preparation: Peel, wash and slice the potatoes. Cook them with salt and broken up bay leaves until they are tender.
Cooking: Make a pale golden *roux* with the oil and flour, mix in the peeled and finely chopped onion, dilute it with a little cold water and add to the potatoes, stirring all the time. Flavor with vinegar, sugar, and sour cream. Let the mixture boil for a few minutes.

Potatoes with onion

2 lbs / 1 kg potatoes, 8 oz / 250 g onions, 5 tbsp oil,
2 cloves garlic, 1 heaped tsp salt, half tsp ground black pepper

Preparation: Wash and cook the potatoes whole in their skins the day before. Peel and refrigerate them for the night. Next day grate the potatoes on the coarse side of the grater.
Cooking: Peel and very finely chop onion. Fry in oil until golden brown, season with salt, add crushed garlic and black pepper. Keep stirring to prevent burning. Finally mix in the cooked grated potatoes and heat through.

Gánica

2 lbs / 1 kg potatoes, 3-4 tbsp flour, 2 tbsp lard or oil,
1 tsp salt; for topping: fried onions

Preparation: Peel and cut the potatoes into cubes. Cook in just enough salted water to cover.
Cooking: Mash the boiled potatoes with their cooking liquid. Heat the lard or oil in a non-stick frying pan, and add the mashed potatoes. Sprinkle with flour and fry for 15-20 minutes, stirring all the while. Spread this mash evenly into an oiled baking tray and bake in a medium oven until it forms a crust. Sprinkle with the fried onions and serve hot.
For the fried onions: fry three sliced or chopped onions in lard, add 1 tsp paprika and salt.

Potato *prósza*

1.5 lbs / 750 g potatoes, 5-6 oz / 150-200 g flour,
1 cup sour cream, 1 large onion, 2 eggs, 1 level tbsp salt,
black pepper to taste; for the topping: 5 oz / 150 g finely chopped cracklings;
for the baking tray: 2 tbsp lard or oil, 2 tbsp breadcrumbs

Preparation: Peel, wash and grate the potatoes. Peel and finely chop the onion, beat the eggs with the sour cream.

Cooking: Mix the grated potatoes and chopped onion into the egg mixture, season well. Add enough flour to get a very thick batter. Spread this mixture into an oiled baking tray and sprinkle it with the cracklings. Bake in a preheated hot oven until golden brown. Serve cut into squares.

Paprika potatoes in a kettle

2 lbs / 1 kg potatoes, 4 oz / 100 g smoked bacon,
1 large onion, 2 green bell peppers, 1 tomato, 1 tbsp paprika,
half tsp ground black pepper, salt

Preparation: Finely chop the smoked bacon and the onion, peel and dice the potatoes. Remove the seeds from the peppers. Slice the seeded peppers and the tomato.

Cooking: Place the bacon in a kettle and heat until the fat runs, gently fry the chopped onion. Add salt and stir, add paprika and 3 tbsp water. Add the potato cubes and pepper slices, pour in enough water to cover, plus half an inch. Cook until tender, shaking the kettle once in a while. Finally add the sliced tomato. The dish is ready when the sauce turns thick.

Note: You may add sliced wiener wurst or smoked sausages to the potatoes towards the end of the cooking time.

Lecsó cooked over an open fire

3 lbs / 1.25 kg green bell peppers
(you can add a few hot chilies if you like),
4-5 tomatoes, 2 large onions, 4 oz / 100 g smoked bacon,
1 small smoked sausage or wiener wurst, 1 tbsp paprika,
2 cloves garlic, salt to taste

Preparation: Dice the smoked bacon small, and fry it in the kettle until the fat runs. Add the finely chopped onion, and fry until pale golden. Mix in the seeded and sliced bell peppers. Fry peppers until they become translucent, stirring all the time.

Cooking: Sprinkle with paprika, add sliced sausage, chopped tomatoes, and crushed garlic. (If your *lecsó* party takes place in the summer time you can add more tomatoes. If it is later in the year, tomatoes can be sour, so less is enough). Let it boil for 5-6 minutes stirring a few times.

CHICKEN PAPRIKA

FISH DISHES

Fish soup

(for 6)

1 lb / 500 g fish head, fin, tail, and bones, or small fish,
2 lb / 1 kg fish fillets (all this can be obtained from one 4 lb / 2 kg carp),
14 oz / 400 g onions, 3 green bell peppers, half cup dry red wine,
2 cloves garlic, 1 tbsp each salt and paprika, 1 tsp oil;
2 oz / 50 g small square pasta

Preparation: For the fish stock, place all the fish cuttings (or small fish) into a deep pot. Set the milk and roe aside. Add the sliced onions, crushed garlic and half the paprika. Pour in 5 pints / 2.5 liters water, and 1 heaped tsp salt. Let it come to a boil and cook uncovered for at least two hours. Push the mixture through a fine sieve and let it stand for 10 minutes.

Cooking: Mix this thick stock base with enough water to get approximately 3 pints / 1.5 liters. Let it come to a boil and carefully add salted fish fillets one by one. Add the fish milk, roe and pasta. Add slices of green bell pepper and cook for 10 minutes. Heat the oil in another small pot, remove from the heat for a minute to add the remaining paprika. Immediately pour in the red wine and let it boil thoroughly. Add this liquid to the fish soup.

Note: Fish soup must not be stirred, only shaken to prevent the fish fillets from breaking up! Serve piping hot with a few hot chilies at hand to please those who prefer spicier food.

Catfish stew

2 lbs / 800 g catfish fillets, 2 large onions, 2 green bell peppers,
2 tomatoes, 1 cup sour cream, 2 oz / 50 g smoked bacon, 1 tbsp paprika,
1 tsp flour, salt to taste

Preparation: Chop the smoked bacon very finely and fry until its fat runs. Dice the fish fillets. Finely chop the onion, slice the peppers and tomatoes. Mix the sour cream with the flour.
Cooking: Fry the chopped onion in the bacon fat, remove from the heat for a minute to add the paprika, and stir. Add 1 tbsp of water, season with salt and continue cooking. Once hot, place the fish fillet pieces, bell pepper and tomato slices into the pan. Fry for a minute, pour in half cup of water and cook covered for 10-15 minutes. You must not stir, but only shake the pan because fish is delicate and can easily fall apart. Add the sour cream and flour mixture and let it boil for a few minutes over a low flame. It is ready when the paprika sauce rises to the top. The traditional garnish for catfish stew is small flour dumplings.

Layered fish with sauerkraut

1.5 lb / 700 g sauerkraut, 1 lb / 500 g white fish fillets, 8 oz / 250 g tomatoes,
1.5 cups sour cream, 2 cooking apples, 4 oz / 100 g smoked bacon,
2 large onions, 2-3 tbsp flour, salt and ground black pepper to taste

Preparation: Thinly slice the fish fillets and season with salt. Finely chop the smoked bacon and heat until the fat runs. Use half the fat to sauté the peeled and sliced onion. Add the squeezed sauerkraut and cook until tender. (If the sauerkraut is too sour rinse it out in cold water before using).
Cooking: Spread half the onion-sauerkraut mixture into a baking tray. Slice the cored but unpeeled apples and place on top, then spread the other half of the sauerkraut mixture over the apples. Dip the fish slices into flour and brown them quickly on both sides in the bacon fat. Spread a layer of fish on top of the sauerkraut, cover it with a layer of sliced tomatoes and sprinkle it with well-seasoned sour cream. Bake in a preheated medium oven for half an hour.

Barbecued paprika bream

2 lbs / 1 kg of small whole bream, 4 tbsp flour, 4 tbsp oil,
1 tbsp paprika, 1 tsp salt, half tsp ground black pepper

Preparation: Wash, scale and gut the fish, season with salt and let it stand for 30 minutes. Meanwhile mix the paprika and black pepper with the flour. Dip each piece of fish into the seasoned flour, brush them with oil and place on a hot, oiled barbecue. Cook one side, then turn them over, brush with oil again and barbecue until crisp and golden brown.

MEAT DISHES

Pörkölt stews

Suckling pig pörkölt

1.5 lbs / 700 g suckling pig shoulder with skin,
1 large onion, 2 green bell peppers, 2 tomatoes, 1 slice celeriac,
1 tbsp each oil and paprika,
1 tsp salt, half tsp caraway seeds

Preparation: Wash and pat dry the meat. Dice, leaving the skin on. Peel and finely chop the onion and grate the celeriac. Slice the bell peppers and tomatoes.
Cooking: Heat the oil and sauté the onion until pale golden. Remove from the heat for a minute to add the paprika and 2 tbsp of water. Mix and continue cooking. Add the cubed meat and brown for a few minutes. Pour in 1 glass of water, add the bell peppers, the grated celeriac and the caraway seeds. Cover and cook over a low heat, stirring often until the meat becomes tender. Finally add the tomatoes. If the water evaporates too quickly during cooking, add a little more hot water at a time to replace it. The sauce of suckling pig pörkölt has to be quite thick. Serve with pasta pellets.

Pork pörkölt

1 lb / 500 g pork shoulder, 1 large onion,
2 green bell peppers, 1 tomato, 3 tbsp oil, 1 clove garlic,
1 level tbsp paprika, 1 tbsp salt

Preparation: Peel and finely chop the onion and sauté in hot oil together with the crushed garlic. Remove from the heat for a minute while adding the paprika, salt and 2 tbsp of water.

Cooking: Continue cooking, add the pork cubes and sear them on all sides while stirring all the time. Season with salt and gradually pour in 1 cup of water; 1 tbsp at a time, just enough to make sure the meat will brown but not burn. Cover and cook until half done. Mix in the slices of tomato and pepper. Cook until the meat is completely tender.

Pig trotters pörkölt

6 pig trotters, 2 onions, 2 green bell peppers,
1 tomato, 3 tbsp oil, 1 tbsp each paprika (hot if you like),
bouillon powder, salt, pepper

Preparation: Place the cleaned pig trotters into a pressure cooker and add 1 large cup of lightly salted water. Cook until very tender. Remove the trotters from the cooking liquid and discard all the bones. (They should slide off very easily.) Set the meat and the cooking liquid aside. Slice the peppers and the tomato. Peel and finely chop the onions.
Cooking: Sauté the onions in oil, remove from the heat while adding the paprika, bouillon powder and black pepper. Add 2 tbsp of cooking liquid and continue cooking. (At this stage peeled and quartered potatoes may be added to the dish.) Add the boned and diced meat, bell peppers and tomato. Fry for a few minutes, then pour in all the cooking liquid. Cover and boil for ten minutes. (Twenty if you have added potatoes.)

Beef pörkölt in red wine
(Prepared in a kettle)

1.5 lbs / 600 g beef leg, 2 cups dry red wine,
4 oz / 100 g smoked bacon, 2 green bell peppers,
2 large onions, 1 tomato, 1 tbsp paprika, pinch caraway seeds,
salt and black pepper to taste

Preparation: Place the finely diced bacon at the bottom of the kettle and heat until the fat runs. Add the finely chopped onions and sauté until pale golden, stirring all the time. Add the diced beef and sear the meat on all sides.

Cooking: Sprinkle the meat with paprika, mix well, and add 1 large cup of water and 1.5 cups of wine. Season with salt and pepper, add the caraway seeds and cook slowly until it is half done. Pour in the remaining wine, add the bell peppers and tomato. Cook until the sauce thickens and the meat becomes tender. You can add a few hot chilies if you like.

Transylvanian mutton pörkölt

2 lbs / 800 g diced mutton, 4 oz / 100 g smoked bacon,
1 cup red wine, 1 large onion, 1 heaped tbsp lard, 1 tbsp paprika,
1 tbsp salt, 1 clove garlic, a few caraway seeds

Preparation: Finely chop the smoked bacon and fry in the lard. Cut the meat into small cubes. Remove the crisp bacon bits from the fat. Sauté the finely chopped onion in the bacon fat, remove from heat while adding the paprika and the red wine.
Cooking: Add the meat to the onion and wine, season and cook covered until tender. Serve sprinkled with the crisp fried bacon bits.

Paprikás dishes

Chicken paprika

1 whole chicken, 1 cup sour cream, 2 green bell peppers, 1 large onion, 1 tomato,
2 oz / 50 g smoked bacon, 1 tbsp paprika, 1 tsp flour, 1 clove garlic, 1 tsp salt

Preparation: Cut the chicken into portions, (legs, wings and back in half, breast in four), season and set aside. Dice the smoked bacon small, and fry until the fat runs. Slice the bell peppers and cut the tomato into thin wedges. Mix the sour cream with 1 tbsp of water and flour until smooth.
Cooking: Finely chop the peeled onion and sauté in the bacon fat until translucent. Remove from the heat while adding the paprika and 2 tbsp of water. Continue cooking and brown all the chicken pieces on both sides. Add the bell peppers and tomato. Cover and cook in its own

juices on a low flame. If it gets too dry add 1-2 tbsp of hot water at a time. Finally mix in the sour cream, shake the pan a few times and cook until the red paprika sauce rises to the top. (It is not advisable to stir it too much because tender chicken meat call easily fall apart.) Serve with traditional flour or curd cheese dumplings.

Chicken liver paprika

1 lb / 500 g chicken liver, 4 green bell peppers, 2 large onions, 2 tomatoes,
4 oz / 100 g smoked bacon, half cup sour cream, 3 cloves garlic, 1 tsp paprika,
1 level tsp salt, black pepper and marjoram to taste

Preparation: Finely dice the smoked bacon and fry until the fat runs. Set aside 2 tbsp of the fat. Sauté the peeled and thinly sliced onions in the bacon fat, remove from heat while adding the paprika, mix well and add 2 tbsp of water. Put it back on the flame. Add the sliced bell peppers, salt, pepper and marjoram, cover and steam until translucent. Meanwhile clean the chicken livers and cut them into thin slices.

Cooking: Heat the 2 tbsp of reserved fat in a non-stick frying pan and fry the liver pieces stirring all the time until they turn light in color. Keep it warm. Add the crushed garlic to the pepper-tomato mixture and cook until the tomato pieces collapse a little. Add the chicken liver, turn off the heat and mix in the sour cream.

Note: Everyone should season the dish on their plates because salt makes the liver harden during cooking!

Summer pork stew

1.5 lbs / 600 g pork shoulder, 8 oz / 250 g mushrooms,
8 oz / 250 g mixed color bell peppers, 1 large onion, 1 large tomato, 1 cup sour cream,
4 tbsp oil, 2 cloves garlic, 1 tsp flour, 1 tsp paprika, salt to taste

Preparation: Heat the oil and sauté the peeled and finely chopped onion. Remove from the heat to add the paprika and 2 tbsp of water. Continue cooking. Add the thinly sliced pork shoulder and fry until all the pieces turn white. Add the peeled and sliced mushrooms and the seeded and chopped peppers.

Cooking: Cook covered until almost done, stirring once in a while. Add the crushed garlic and sliced tomato, cook until the meat is completely tender. Mix the flour with the sour cream and add to the stew to thicken. Let it come to a boil stirring continuously. Serve with boiled potatoes.

Knuckle of ham paprika

1 large boned knuckle of ham with skin, 2 large onions,
2 green bell peppers, 2 tomatoes, half cup sour cream, 2 tbsp oil,
1 tbsp paprika (it can be hot if you like), 2 cloves garlic,
salt to taste

Preparation: Clean and wash the knuckle of ham, dry, and dice small. leaving the skin on. Peel and finely chop the onions, slice the bell peppers and tomatoes.

Cooking: Heat the oil in a pressure cooker and sauté the onions until translucent, sprinkle with paprika. Add the meat and brown, stirring all the time. Add the bell peppers, tomatoes and crushed garlic, season and pour in 1 cup of water. Seal the pressure cooker, let it come to a boil and cook for 40 minutes. Mix in the sour cream, stir everything well and serve piping hot.

Note: This dish is far from diet food but it tastes so delicious that it is worth giving yourself a guilt free treat once a year!

Lamb paprika with rosemary

2 lbs / 1 kg lamb, 1 cup sour cream, 2 onions,
2 green bell peppers, 1 tomato, 1 sprig fresh rosemary (or 1 tsp dried),
3 tbsp oil, 1 tbsp paprika, salt to taste

Preparation: Wash the meat, pat dry and dice. Peel and chop the onions. Seed and thinly slice the bell peppers, cut the tomato into wedges. Finely chop the fresh rosemary.

BEAN GOULASH

Cooking: Heat the oil in a frying pan, sauté the onions, remove from the heat while adding half the paprika, mix quickly and add 2 tbsp of water. Continue cooking. Add the lamb pieces and fry until they are cooked on all sides. Mix in the bell peppers and tomato, fry for another 2 minutes. Finally sprinkle with the remaining paprika and rosemary, mix quickly, cover and cook for about 50 minutes. When the meat is tender add the sour cream mixed with salt and flour. Let it come to the boil again, then turn off the heat, but keep covered for 15 minutes. Serve with small dumplings or boiled potatoes.

Rabbit stew with paprika

1 whole rabbit, 1 cup dry white wine, 1 cup sour cream,
4 oz / 100 g smoked bacon, 2 green bell peppers, 1 large onion,
1 tomato, 1 very small celeriac bulb, 1 clove garlic,
1 tsp paprika, 1 tsp flour, salt to taste

Preparation: Wash the rabbit, pat dry and cut into smallish pieces. Finely chop the peeled onion, thinly slice the smoked bacon and fry until the fat runs. Chop the bell peppers and tomato, peel and grate the celeriac.

Cooking: Gently fry the onions and celeriac in the smoked bacon fat until the onions turn translucent. Remove from the heat, mix in the paprika, and immediately add 2 tbsp of water. Continue cooking and add the rabbit pieces. Season and sear the meat on all sides. Pour in half cup of water and half cup of wine, cover and cook until tender. If the liquid evaporates too quickly replace it by adding the remaining wine bit by bit. Finally add the bell peppers and tomato, and thicken with the sour cream mixed with flour. Let it boil for 5 more minutes and serve with small dumplings or boiled potatoes.

Note: If you prefer to serve boneless pieces you can easily bone the rabbit once it is completely tender.

STUFFED CABBAGE
BAKED IN SOUR CREAM

Goulashes

Beef goulash

1.5 lbs / 600 g beef, 1 lb / 500 g peeled potatoes,
12 oz / 300 g mixed stock vegetables,
(4 oz / 100 g each carrots, parsnips and celeriac bulb)
1 large onion, 2 green bell peppers, 1 tomato, 3 tbsp oil,
1 level tbsp paprika (if you like it hot use a little hot paprika paste),
1 level tbsp salt, 1 clove garlic, 1 pinch ground caraway

Preparation: Wash, pat dry and dice the meat. Dice the peeled potatoes and thinly slice the vegetables. Wash, seed and slice the peppers into rings, cut the tomatoes into thin wedges.
Cooking: Heat the oil and gently sauté the peeled and finely chopped onion. Remove from the heat to mix in the paprika and 2 tbsp of water. Continue cooking. Add the diced meat and fry on all sides, stirring. Pour in 3 pints / 1.5 liters of water, and cook until the meat is half done, then add the washed and chopped vegetables and potatoes. Season with salt and caraway and cook until everything becomes tender. Add the bell peppers and tomato and cook for 2 more minutes.
Note: Add hot paprika paste at the end of cooking time. If one of your guests or family members does not like spicy food, add a tiny amount to individual plates when you serve. The hot soup will immediately merge with the 'heat'.

Kettle goulash
cooked over an open fire

(for 6)

2 lbs / 1 kg beef leg, 8 oz / 1 kg potatoes, 2 cups dry red wine,
4 large onions, 4 green bell peppers, 2 tomatoes, 4 oz / 100 g smoked bacon,
2 tbsp paprika, 1 tbsp salt, pinch caraway, black pepper to taste

Preparation: Place the finely chopped smoked bacon in the bottom of the kettle, and heat until the fat runs. Add the peeled and very finely chopped onions and sauté until pale golden, stirring all the time. Add the cubed beef and fry on all sides.

Cooking: Sprinkle with paprika, mix well and pour in 1 large cup of water and 1.5 cups of wine. Season with salt and pepper, add the caraway and gently cook until half done. Gradually pour in the remaining wine, add the peeled and chopped potatoes and sliced bell peppers and tomatoes. Cook until all the ingredients are tender. If you like spicy food you can add some hot chili peppers.

Note: Cooking kettle goulash can take up to three hours. If you want to speed up the process you can cook a beef pörkölt in a pressure cooker, pour it into the kettle, add potatoes and finish the goulash outdoors.

Székely goulash

(for 6)

1.5 lbs / 750 g sauerkraut, 1.5 lbs / 750 g pork shoulder or leg,
1.5 cups sour cream, 1 large onion, 2 green bell peppers,
1 tomato, 1 tbsp paprika, 1 tbsp flour, 2 tbsp lard,
1 tsp dried savory, half tsp ground caraway, salt to taste

Preparation: Dice the meat. Sauté the peeled and finely chopped onion in 1.5 tbsp of lard until pale golden. Add the meat and fry quickly over a high heat. Sprinkle with paprika, and pour in 2 cups of water. Cook covered, stirring occasionally, until half done.

Cooking: While the meat is cooking, fry the drained sauerkraut in the remaining half tbsp of lard. Pour in the sauerkraut liquid and 1 cup of water, then cook until half done. Mix the partially cooked meat and sauerkraut and continue cooking them together until the meat becomes tender. Add the seeded and sliced peppers and tomatoes and thicken with a mixture of half cup water, 1 cup of sour cream and flour. Bring to the boil, stirring all the time. Serve sprinkled with the remaining sour cream and decorated with tomato slices.

Bean goulash

(for 8)

2 lbs / 1 kg beef leg, 1 lb / 400 g dried beans,
2 lbs / 1 kg potatoes, 1 lb / 400 g mixed stock vegetables,
2 large onions, 2 green bell peppers, 2 tomatoes,
2 bay leaves, 4 cloves garlic, 2 tbsp paprika, 2 tbsp salt

Preparation: Soak the beans overnight. Next day dice the meat. Peel and dice the potatoes. Peel and slice the stock vegetables. Chop the bell peppers and tomatoes finely.

Cooking: Heat the oil and sauté the onions until transparent. Add the diced meat, sprinkle with paprika, stir and pour in 2 pints / 1 liter of water. Add the crushed garlic, bay leaves, and salt and cook until the meat is almost tender. Add the drained pre-soaked beans. Add more water to cover the beans and the meat completely. When both are tender, add stock vegetables and potatoes and continue cooking on a low heat until everything is well done.

Chicken goulash in a kettle

1 medium chicken, 1.5 lbs / 500 g potatoes, 2 large onions,
2 green bell peppers, 2 tomatoes, 1 tbsp paprika, 2 cloves garlic,
3 tbsp oil, salt to taste

Preparation: Peel and finely chop the onions, slice the peppers and tomatoes. Cut the chicken into portions, peel and dice the potatoes.

Cooking: Heat the oil in a kettle and sauté the chopped onions until they become translucent. Mix in the paprika and salt and 3 tbsp of water. Put in the chicken pieces in a single layer. Pour in enough water to cover the chicken. Add the peeled and crushed garlic and season well. Let it come to the boil and cook for 25 minutes. Do not stir because tender chicken pieces can easily fall apart, only shake the kettle. Add the potatoes and green peppers. Add more water to cover the potatoes and chicken, cook for 20 minutes more and then add the tomatoes. Let it boil for another few minutes, then remove from the heat and let it stand for 10 minutes before serving.

Ham goulash

1 lb / 500 g piece raw, boneless smoked ham,
1 lb / 500 g potatoes, 8 oz / 250 g prunes, 2 large onions,
1 cup sour cream, 4 tbsp oil, half tsp ground black pepper,
2 whole cardamom pods, 2 crushed cloves,
milk for soaking ham

Preparation: Place the ham in enough milk to cover it and soak overnight, covered in the fridge. Next day drain the ham and dice small. Peel the potatoes and onions and chop finely.
Cooking: Heat the oil and sauté the onions until pale golden, add the ham pieces and cook for a few minutes. Pour in 3 pints / 1.5 liters of water and cook over a low heat until tender. Add the potatoes, prunes and spices. (Remove small black seeds from cardamom pods, add to the dish and discard the outer skin). When the potatoes are soft, add sour cream. Season if necessary. (But beware! Ham is salty so this soup should only be seasoned when it is completely ready). Let it boil for a few more minutes. It is a rich and very tasty soup that can serve as a main meal.

Mutton goulash

2 lbs / 1 kg bony mutton, 1.5 lbs / 650 g potatoes,
1 cup dry red wine, 2 medium onions, 1 green bell pepper,
1 tomato, small hot chili pepper, 2 tbsp oil,
1 tbsp each paprika and salt, 3 cloves garlic,
2 fl oz / 50 ml vinegar

Preparation: Remove the tendons, fat and bones from the mutton. Dice the meat also chopping up the bones. Peel and cut the potatoes lengthwise into wedges. Peel and finely chop the onions, sauté in oil. Remove from the heat, mix in the paprika and 2 tbsp of water, continue cooking.
Cooking: Add the mutton and the bones, and brown over a high heat stirring continuously. Pour in 1 cup of water, cover and cook until tender. Replace the liquid once in a while if it evaporates too quickly. Season and add peeled and crushed garlic. Add sliced bell peppers,

hot chilies and potatoes. Pour in enough water to cover it all and cook until the potatoes are done. Add the sliced tomato and wine, then let it boil uncovered until the sauce thickens. Discard the bones before serving and season if necessary.

Note: If you do not like the typical taste and smell of mutton, put the raw meat in enough water to cover with 2 fl oz / 50 ml of vinegar, let it come to a boil, drain and continue cooking the way described above.

Meat dishes with sauerkraut

Stuffed cabbage
baked in sour cream

8 pickled cabbage leaves, 1 lb / 450 g sauerkraut,
1 lb / 400 g boneless pork spare ribs, 3 cups sour cream,
4 oz / 100 g smoked bacon, 4 oz / 100 g rice,
1 small onion, 1 tsp dried savory, 1 tbsp oil,
half tsp paprika, salt and ground black pepper to taste

Preparation: Cook this dish in an earthenware oven proof dish pre-soaked in cold water for 30 minutes before using. Cut out the thick veins from the cabbage leaves. Wash the rice in a colander several times under running cold water and cook in one and a half times more salted water until half done. Cut the smoked bacon into large, very thin slices. Sauté the very finely chopped onion in oil. Mince or dice the meat very small, mix with half the cooked rice, salt, pepper, paprika and sautéed onion.

Cooking: Put an equal amount of the stuffing mixture on each cabbage leaf, roll up, and make eight parcels. Line the earthenware dish with thinly sliced bacon, spread half the sauerkraut over it, sprinkle with half the savory, season with salt and pepper and lay the stuffed parcels on top. Pour half the sour cream all over the top and repeat the same steps. Cover the dish and put it in a cold oven. Start baking in a low oven for 15 minutes, then increase the heat and bake in a medium oven for at least 2.5 hours. (You can bake it in a cast iron pot or in an oven-proof glass dish, but you will need more sour cream.)

Stuffed cabbage Kolozsvár style

(for 8)

1.5 lbs / 600 g pork shoulder, 1 lb / 500 g soft smoked sausage,
2 lbs / 800 g piece boneless pork chop,
1 lb / 500 g smoked ham or spare rib,
3 lbs / 1.5 kg sauerkraut, 16 pickled cabbage leaves,
5 oz / 150 g lard, 2 onions, 2 cloves garlic,
7 oz / 200 g rice, 2 eggs, 3 cups + 1 cup sour cream, black pepper,
dried marjoram, paprika and salt to taste

Preparation: Soak the smoked ham overnight. Mince half of the spare rib, mix with the peeled and grated onions, washed and drained rice, beaten eggs, salt, pepper, marjoram and paprika. Cut out the thickest veins from the cabbage leaves and stuff them with the mince and rice mixture. Fold up the two ends to make neat parcels. Slice the smoked ham, sausage and pork chop into 8 portions. Rub the lard all over the inside of a large, oven proof earthenware dish that had been soaked in cold for an hour.

Cooking: Spread quarter of the sauerkraut evenly in the bottom of the dish. Season and place the stuffed parcels on top. Put another layer of cabbage over the sauerkraut followed by a layer of ham slices and sauerkraut again. Scatter the smoked sausage slices on top and cover with another layer of sauerkraut. Sprinkle with crushed garlic, 3 cups of sour cream, and cover the dish with its own pre-soaked lid. Start cooking in a cold oven, and cook for 3 hours over a moderate heat. Fry the pork chops in a little oil and serve the stuffed cabbage dish topped with the pork chops. Mix the remaining sour cream with a little paprika and sprinkle on top.

Hen in sauerkraut liquid
with horseradish

half a hen, 2 pints / 1 liter sauerkraut liquid,
(or liquid from pickled vegetables diluted with water),
1 fresh horseradish, half cup single cream, half cup sour cream,
1 tbsp flour, salt and sugar to taste

Preparation: Cut the hen into small portions. Mix the cream, sour cream and flour. Cut out a little fat from under the hen's skin, heat and brown the hen pieces in it on both sides.
Cooking: Pour the sauerkraut liquid over the hen, season well and cook until tender. Lift the hen out of the liquid, remove all the bones and cut the meat into small strips. Boil the cooking liquid mixed with the cream, sour cream and flour. Peel and grate the horseradish, and sprinkle half on top of the dish. Serve with the other half on the side.

Hen ragout with cabbage

1.5 lb / 700 g hen, 1 small white cabbage,
7 oz / 200 g cooked, smoked ham, 1 large onion,
1 cup dry white wine, 1 cup sour cream,
1 bunch parsley, 2 oz / 50 g smoked bacon, 3 tbsp oil,
salt and black pepper to taste

Preparation: Discard any excess fat and skin from the hen, bone and dice the meat. Peel and sauté the chopped onion in oil, add the diced hen. Brown on all sides and pour in 1 small cup of water. Season well and cook covered until tender.
Cooking: Dice the cabbage and sauté in finely chopped smoked bacon fat, covered, stirring occasionally. When the hen is tender, add the cabbage and the finely chopped smoked ham. Pour in the wine and let it come to the boil. Thicken the ragout with sour cream and flour mixed with half cup of water. Let it boil for 6-7 minutes, sprinkle with chopped parsley and serve with large semolina dumplings.

Duck with cabbage

(for 5)

1 small duck, 1.5 lbs / 750 g sauerkraut,
2 large onions, 2 cups sour cream,
1 hot chili pepper, 3 cloves garlic, 1 tsp savory,
1 bay leaf, half tsp ground black pepper, salt to taste;
1 tbsp oil for the baking tray

Preparation: Cut the duck into small portions (legs in half, breast in half both ways, back and wings in half). Season the duck pieces well. Oil a baking tray big enough to hold the duck pieces in a single layer.

Cooking: Spread the sauerkraut in the bottom of the baking tray. Sprinkle with savory, slices of chili pepper and onion. Season well. Scatter the broken bay leaf and place the duck pieces on top. Score the duck skin with a sharp knife. Cover and bake in a preheated medium oven for 1.5 hours. Take out the tender duck pieces and put them aside. Place the sauerkraut in a colander and let it drip until all fat has drained out. Spread the almost dry sauerkraut in another baking dish. Place the duck pieces with the skin side on top. Mix the crushed garlic into the sour cream, season with salt and pepper and brush it over the duck skins. Put it back into the oven and bake uncovered until crispy and golden brown.

Note: You can keep the left-over fatty juice in the fridge and gradually use it for other dishes.

Goose stuffed with sauerkraut

(for 8)

1 goose, 8 oz / 250 g sauerkraut, 2 tart apples,
1 large onion, 2 tbsp uncooked rice, half cup red wine,
1 tsp marjoram, half tsp ground caraway, salt to taste

Preparation: Chop sauerkraut into small pieces. Add to it peeled and finely chopped onion, washed and uncooked rice, peeled, cored and grated apples, salt, marjoram and caraway. Mix everything well and stuff it into the washed and salted cavity of the goose. Hold up the goose and pour red wine into the cavity. Within a few minutes it will filter through the stuffing into the cavity. Sew opening together tightly to prevent any stuffing leaking out. Slit the duck skin every 2 mm, season with salt and place it in a large baking tray.

Cooking: Pour 2 cups of water into the baking tray and cover. Put it in a preheated medium oven and bake for at least 2.5 hours. Once the goose is tender, remove cover and roast on both sides until crispy and golden brown. Discard the greasy juice, carve the goose, and serve surrounded by the sauerkraut stuffing.

Pork chops Csíkszereda style

1.5 lbs / 600 g boneless, sliced pork chops,
1.5 lbs / 600 g sauerkraut, 1 large onion, 3 green bell peppers,
2 tomatoes, 1 cup sour cream, 4 tbsp oil, 1 bunch fresh tarragon,
1 tsp paprika, 3 cloves garlic, half tsp ground caraway, pinch sugar,
salt to taste, ground black pepper; 2 portions cooked rice

Preparation: Sauté peeled and chopped onion in 3 tbsp oil, and brown flattened chops on both sides. Remove from frying pan and set aside. Add paprika, sliced tomatoes, and seeded and sliced bell peppers to pan, pour in half cup water and let it boil. Mix in 1 crushed clove garlic and black pepper, lay pork chops on top and cook over a low heat, covered, until tender. If liquid evaporates too quickly replace it with 1 tbsp water at a time.

Cooking: While the meat is cooking, brown sauerkraut in remaining oil, add caraway, finely chopped tarragon leaves, salt and remaining 2 cloves of crushed garlic. Cover and cook until soft, adding a pinch sugar. If the sauerkraut gets too dry, moisten it with 1 tbsp water at a time. Mix in cooked rice (leftover rice is good) and spread the mixture into an ovenproof dish. Place pork chops over sauerkraut and top it with a mixture of sour cream and meat juices. Heat it in the oven and serve with raw slices of green pepper and sour cream.

Háromszéki leg of pork

8 small slices pork leg, 8 pickled cabbage leaves,
2 cups sour cream, 2 large tart apples,
1 large onion, 1 tsp paprika (hot if you like), half tsp savory,
1 clove of garlic, salt and pepper to taste

Preparation: Flatten the meat slices, season and wrap each one individually in a cabbage leaf. Peel and chop onion.

Cooking: Place parcels in an ovenproof dish, surround them with peeled and thinly sliced apples, scatter onion pieces over the top, add savory and crushed garlic. Mix sour cream with salt and paprika and pour over dish. Add half cup water, cover with aluminum foil and bake in a preheated hot oven for 80 minutes.

Smoked ham shank
with sauerkraut

1 large ham shank, 8 oz / 250 g sauerkraut,
1 large quince, 1 cup sour cream, 1 large onion,
1 bunch fresh dill, 2 oz / 50 g smoked bacon,
1 tsp paprika, salt and pepper to taste

Preparation: Clean ham shank and cut into thin slices together leaving the skin on. Finely dice and fry the smoked bacon.

Cooking: Sauté the peeled and finely chopped onion in bacon fat, remove from heat, mix in paprika, salt, 2 tbsp water and add ham slices. Brown on all sides and pour in 1 large cup of water. Cook until tender. If the liquid evaporates too quickly during cooking, replace it with a little hot water at a time. Add sauerkraut, as well as peeled, cored and thinly sliced quince. Cook together until everything is well done, finally add finely chopped dill and ground black pepper. Serve topped with sour cream.

Stuffed pork Vecsés style

(for 7-8)

1.5 lbs / 750 g lean thin flank of pork,
1 lb / 500 g sauerkraut,
1 cup sour cream, 2 oz / 50 g smoked bacon,
1 small onion, 1 egg, 1-2 tbsp breadcrumbs,
1 tbsp prepared mustard, half tsp savory,
2 cloves garlic, salt and pepper to taste

Preparation: Prepare thin pork flank for stuffing: prick it with a pointy, sharp knife, then rub it with salt inside and out. Finely dice the smoked bacon and fry until its fat runs. Remove crispy bits and mix them with beaten egg, chopped and squeezed sauerkraut, mustard, salt, pepper, a pinch of sugar and crushed garlic. Mix in enough breadcrumbs to get a not too runny stuffing.

Cooking: Stuff enough mixture into the meat to get a nice, round piece. Sew the opening together tightly and place the stuffed meat into pan with melted bacon fat. Brown on both sides, and put it into an ovenproof dish. Shape small balls out of the remaining stuffing mixture and place these around the meat. Sprinkle with sour cream, cover the dish and bake it in a preheated oven for 1 hour. Remove cover and brown. Let it rest for 15 minutes before slicing.

Ham with sauerkraut

1 lb / 500 g sauerkraut, 1 lb / 500 g mixed stock vegetables,
1 lb / 400 g uncooked smoked ham,
1.5 cups sour cream, 2 large tart apples,
2 glasses dry white wine, 1 tbsp oil, half tsp dried savory,
1 clove garlic, 3 ground cloves; milk for soaking ham

Preparation: Soak ham overnight in enough milk to cover it. Next day drain and slice into strips. If the sauerkraut is too sour, rinse it in water and let it drain. Peel vegetables and cut them into batons. Peel, core and cut apples into thin strips.

Cooking: Oil a deep ovenproof dish and put half the sauerkraut at the bottom followed by half the ham and apples. Next, put in half the vegetables, the remaining sauerkraut, ham, apple and vegetables. Mix wine with sour cream, savory and cloves, add 1 cup of milk, crushed garlic and pour this liquid over the dish, enough to completely cover the vegetables. If there is not enough liquid, add some more milk. Cover and bake in a preheated medium oven for 2 hours.

Roasts

Roast chicken in a salt crust

2 small chickens, 3 lbs / 1.5 kg salt, 1 apple,
1 tsp marjoram, half tsp ground black pepper

Preparation: Wash and pat dry chickens. Put cored and quartered apple into the cavity of each. Rub it with marjoram and season well.
Cooking: Take an ovenproof dish and pour enough salt at the bottom to cover it. Place chickens on top. Mix remaining salt with a bit of water and cover chickens with salt paste completely. Not an inch of skin must be seen! During roasting the salt paste will turn into a crust and seal all flavor in. Put it into a preheated hot oven for 50 minutes and only break off salt crust at the table. Serve with a green salad.

Transylvanian grilled pork

4 large boneless juicy pork steaks (neck part),
1 oz / 30 g smoked bacon, 1 tbsp prepared mustard,
1 tbsp oil, 3 cloves garlic, pinch ground juniper berries,
salt and pepper to taste

Preparation: Season meat with juniper and black pepper, rub with crushed garlic, oil and mustard, and marinate in fridge for 24 hours. Rub the barbecue with bacon piece several times.

[53]

Cooking: Place pork slices on the hot barbecue and grill for 10-12 minutes. Turn over the slices and repeat. It is delicious served with potatoes, roast pepper salad in vinaigrette, tomato salad with red onions or hot mixed pickles.

Marinated pork steaks

4 large slices boneless pork neck, 1 pint / 500 ml milk,
half cup oil, 3 tbsp flour, 6-7 cloves garlic, 1 tsp paprika,
half tsp ground black pepper, salt to taste

Preparation: Mix salt, pepper and peeled and crushed garlic cloves into milk the day before. Tenderize the meat, put it in a dish and pour spiced milk over. Cover and keep in the fridge for at least 24 hours.
Cooking: Remove pork slices from milk and coat both sides with flour seasoned with black pepper and paprika. Heat oil and brown one side of the meat in a covered pan. Remove lid, turn slices around and brown other side.
Note: The longer the pork slices marinate in the milk the more tender and tastier they become. They'll keep in the fridge for up to three days but they must be tightly covered!

Leg of lamb with garlic

2 lbs / 800 g boneless leg of lamb,
1 head garlic, 2 tbsp oil, 1 tbsp tomato purée,
salt and pepper to taste

Preparation: Peel garlic cloves and cut larger ones into halves. Wash and pat meat dry, then cut small slits into it and fill them with garlic. Tie meat with a string.
Cooking: Heat oil in a frying pan and brown the meat on all sides. Take it out of the pan and fry tomato purée in the meat juice. Put back the lamb, season well and pour in 1 cup water. Cover and cook for approximately 80 minutes. Once tender, lift it out and let it rest for 20 minutes. Slice it at right angles to its fibers, put it back in the pan and heat. Serve with rice and steamed vegetables such as brussel sprouts, carrots and broccoli.

Crispy roast suckling pig

2 lbs / 1 kg boneless leg with skin, 5 cloves garlic,
half cup beer, salt and pepper to taste

Preparation: Wash and pat dry the meat, cut small indentations in the meat and slide peeled and sliced garlic cloves into them, seasoning well. Tie the meat with a string so that the skin is on the outside.

Cooking: Preheat the oven, then place the meat in a baking dish, pour in half a glass of water and first bake in a high oven until it gets a crisp, golden crust. Lower the heat and continue roasting until a fork inserted comes out easily. Turn the meat around a few times while baking and keep brushing it with beer. Slice while it is hot and serve with sautéed cabbage.

Pork chop with sausage

1.5 lbs / 700 g boneless pork chop,
1 small sausage, 2 oz / 50 g smoked bacon,
1 tbsp paprika paste, salt to taste

Preparation: Wash and pat dry the meat. Take a sharp and pointed knife and pierce a hole into the middle of the meat big enough to hold the sausage. Skin the sausage and push it into the meat.

Cooking: Place stuffed meat on a sheet of aluminum foil, lightly season and spread paprika paste all over. Slice smoked bacon very thinly and wrap around meat. Wrap it in foil and bake in a preheated oven for 1 hr 15 minutes. Open the foil parcel and let the meat turn golden brown. Leave it to rest for 10 minutes before carving. Pour cooking juice over it and serve with potatoes and a salad.

Scrumptious roast

1.5 lbs / 800 g leg of pork, 2 oz / 50 g smoked bacon,
2 tbsp oil, 1 tbsp each paprika and prepared mustard,
1 tsp salt, 3 cloves garlic, half tsp each ground caraway
and black pepper

Preparation: Wash and pat dry the meat. Peel and slice garlic cloves into slivers, cut bacon into thin stripes. Mix all the spices with 1 tbsp oil and rub it all over the meat. Prick holes into the meat and slide in garlic slivers and bacon strips. Let it rest for 2-3 hours.
Cooking: Heat the remaining oil and brown the meat on all sides. The browner it turns, the tastier it becomes. Pour in half cup of water, cover and bake in a preheated medium oven. Only remove the cover once the roast is completely tender. Slice before serving with its own scrumptious juice.

Roast pork with tarragon

2 lbs / 1 kg boneless pork shoulder, half cup dry white wine,
half cup tomato juice, 1 onion, 4 tbsp olive oil,
1 bunch fresh tarragon, 4 cloves garlic, salt to taste

Preparation: Wash and pat dry meat, and rub it with salt all over. Peel and finely chop onion and garlic.
Cooking: Heat olive oil and sauté onion and garlic, add meat and brown on all sides. Place meat in a roasting tin, pour in wine and tomato juice and sprinkle with finely chopped tarragon. Roast while basting with juices all the time. Let it rest for 15 minutes before slicing. Serve in its own juices.

Baked knuckle of ham

(for 6)

2 boned knuckles with skin, 2 large onions,
1.5 cups sour cream, 2 green bell peppers,
2 large firm tomatoes, 2 tbsp each flour and oil,
1 tsp hot paprika, half tsp ground black pepper,
6 cloves garlic, salt to taste

Preparation: Soak an unglazed earthenware baking dish with a lid in cold water for 0.5 hour. Cut knuckles into half inch slices. Mix flour, salt, pepper and paprika. Slice onions into rings.
Cooking: Coat both sides of knuckle slices with the seasoned flour. Spread half of the onion rings in the bottom of the earthenware dish and place coated ham slices on top. Cover with the remaining onions, slices of tomatoes and bell peppers. Mix sour cream with oil, salt and crushed garlic, pour over the top. Cover the dish and put it in a cold oven. Turn on the heat and bake for 15 minutes in a low oven. Increase the temperature and bake in a medium oven for 2.5 hours. Remove the lid and brown the top. Serve piping hot.

Garlicky spareribs

2 lbs / 800 g spareribs, half cup sour cream, 3 cloves garlic,
1 tsp flour, salt, caraway and ground black pepper to taste

Preparation: Wash and pat dry the meat, coil it up and steam it in a pressure cooker over half cup of salted water. Wait thirty minutes after the pressure cooker beeps and take out the meat, drain it and bone it. Cut the meat into small pieces and set it aside.
Cooking: Add up to 1 cup of water to the steaming liquid. Mix it with the sour cream, flour and crushed garlic. Let it boil until it thickens. Season with black pepper and boil the meat pieces in this liquid for a few minutes.

Home butchering products

Smoked liver sausage

2 lbs / 1 kg pork liver, 2lbs / 1 kg thin pork flank,
2 onions, 3 oz / 100 g pork dripping,
half tsp each ground allspice and dried marjoram,
salt to taste

Preparation: Cook the meat in salted water until tender, drain and let it cool. Put the chopped liver into the cooking liquid of the meat for a minute until it turns pale. Prick a piece with a fork and if no blood oozes out, drain and mince together with the cooked meat.
Cooking: Sauté the finely chopped onions in the pork dripping until pale golden, add to the minced liver and meat, season with spices and salt, add 3-4 tbsp cooking liquid and mix well. Thoroughly clean and boil intestines and fill with the mixture. Tie 5 inch / 15 cm long sausages in pairs and let them cook in simmering water for 30 minutes. Cool them in cold water and let them dry on wooden boards. Once they are completely dry hang them over cold smoke for 3-4 days. Store them in a cool and airy place hung up in pairs. Smoked liver sausages keep well for months and can be eaten both hot or cold.
Note: Both in the Hungarian provinces and in the environs of Budapest smoke-houses can be found to take home-made sausages to for smoking.

Hungarian pork cheese

1 pig's head, 1 pig's tongue, 5 oz / 150 g bacon skin,
1 pig's stomach, 5 cloves garlic, paprika, black pepper,
salt to taste

Preparation: Wash pig's head thoroughly and burn off any bristles with a blow torch. Discard the eyes. Boil meat, tongue and bacon skin in salted water until very tender. At this point it will be easy to bone the meat. Meanwhile carefully wash the pig's stomach.

Cooking: Dice meat, tongue and bacon skin small. Peel and crush garlic cloves and soak them in 5 tbsp of cooking liquid for 10 minutes. Drain and pour garlic infused liquid over the meat mixture without the actual garlic pieces. Season with the spices and mix well. Fill the mixture tightly into the stomach and stitch it together with thread. Prick a few holes into the stomach with a needle and let it simmer for 1 hour in the cooking liquid. If it is needed add a little water during the cooking time.

Drain and weigh it down between two wooden boards for 24 hours. It keeps for one week in the fridge but if you smoke it over cold smoke for two days it will keep longer.

Note: If you cannot obtain a pig's stomach you can use a form lined with cling film and press the pork cheese into it. 24 hours later you can turn out the pig's cheese in one piece.

Liver paté

1 whole pig's liver, 1/3 of the liver's quantity in smoked bacon,
1 large onion, 1 heaped tbsp lard, 2 cloves garlic, half tsp ground cloves,
salt and pepper to taste

Preparation: Cook the liver in boiling water for five minutes. Drain and put it through the grinder twice. Peel and grate the onion.

Cooking: Sauté the chopped onion in the lard. Dice the bacon small and mix with the spices and the crushed garlic. Loosen the mixture with 1-2 tbsp of the liver's cooking liquid, and fill it into one piece of intestine. Tie it tightly and cook in simmering water for 1 hour. Drain and cool in cold water, then let it dry on a wooden board. When it is completely cold put it the fridge. It keeps for 10 days but if it is smoked over cold smoke it can keep up to three weeks.

Note: If intestines are not available the mixture can be stuffed into a ring cake tin and baked in the oven in a *bain-marie*. (A bain-marie means putting a tray of water at the bottom of the oven to create steam during baking.)

Roast blood or liver sausages

These sausages are not exactly slimming, although they are only fattening if they are prepared in the wrong way. It is a bad habit to fry sausages in a lot of lard because it only increases their fat content. Rather, wrap the sausages in aluminum foil without using any extra fat. Place them under a hot grill or in the oven and roast for ten minutes on each side. All the excess fat will come out and can be discarded at the end. If the intestines are unblemished the stuffing will not ooze out as long as you do not prick them with a fork. Use two spatulas and be careful when turning them around.

Sausage making

Sausage meat must never be washed because it will soak up water and spoil more easily. Blood must be wiped off with a clean cloth. Remove all the sinewy and gristly parts because they cannot be minced and there is nothing worse than a very chewy sausage!

The best cuts for sausage making are boned neck, shoulder, flank, or leg of pork. Certain sausage varieties require the addition of beef as well. If the sausage is made from bony meat please note that the measurements given in the recipes are for the net weight!

The weight loss of sausages after smoking and drying, depending on the water content of the meat, is about 3-4% per 2 lbs / 1 kilo. This means that 12 lbs / 6 kg of raw sausages will become 5 kg / 700 g. This weight will further decrease during drying and storing time. The thinner the intestine that holds the stuffing, the more water it loses.

One of the most important rules of sausage making is that the raw sausage has to be compact enough to be handled without it falling apart or leaking. If you notice any air bubbles inside the ready filled sausage mixture prick them with a needle but make sure not to prick too many holes because the intestine can rupture.

This time do not use string to tie the ends but twist one end of the intestine around and fill it tightly with the stuffing mix. Keep coiling up the long, 'endless' sausage carefully on the table until you reach the end of the intestine. Twist this around again to secure the end. Make twists in 30 cm intervals. This way you will end up with 3-4 pairs of sausages made from a 2-2.5 meter long intestine. You can break it up at the twists or leave it in one long piece. Hang up the sausages on a bar to dry. They will not fall down because the intestines are very elastic when they are wet.

Fresh white pepper sausage

5 lbs / 2.5 kg lean pork meat,
2 oz / 60 g salt, half oz / 15 g white pepper

Preparation: Bone the meat, remove cartilage, sinew and gristle, and grind the meat coarsely. Take very good care not to leave any bone splinters in it. Season with salt and pepper, mix well. Fill the mixture into a thin piece of intestine and put it in the fridge. It will keep for three days raw but if fried it can be kept and eaten for up to a week, and it can be frozen for three months.

Garlicky cured sausage

(makes approx. 22 lbs / 10 kg)

18 lbs / 9 kg pork meat, 2 lbs / 1 kg lean beef,
10 oz / 260 g salt, 2 oz / 60 g sweet paprika,
1 oz / 25 g garlic, 1 level tbsp icing sugar,
1 tbsp dried marjoram, 1 tbsp potassium nitrate,
1.5 oz / 4 g ground white pepper

Preparation: Discard all the sinew, gristle and membrane from the meat and put it through a coarse grinder. Peel and crush garlic cloves and liquidize with half cup of water.
Sprinkle the herbs over the meat, pour in garlic purée, mix and knead well together. Let the mixture rest in a cool place overnight and stuff it into thin intestines. Twist the intestines to create even sized pairs, and smoke them for three days over cold smoke. It can be eaten after three weeks of resting. It is a delicious sausage that keeps for 8-9 months.
Note: Potassium nitrate can be obtained from chemists.

Goose feast

Goose cracklings

goose fat and skin, 1-2 tbsp milk,
salt to taste

Preparation: Cut goose fat and skin into squares and cut slits into each one so that the fat can run freely during roasting.
Cooking: Pour just enough water over the pieces to cover them and cook under a lid until the fat rises to the top. Remove the lid and fry the goose pieces until they turn golden brown and quite crisp. Turn off the heat, sprinkle the pieces with milk and cover immediately. Be careful when sprinkling because the hot fat can burn you. Wait for a few minutes and drain off all the free running fat. Put the cracklings onto a slotted spoon and gently squeeze out the remaining fat. Season with salt while still hot. Cracklings are delicious eaten warm, or cold with crusty bread and thinly sliced red onions!

Roast goose liver

1 fattened goose liver, 3 oz / 90 g goose fat,
1 clove garlic, salt to taste

Preparation: Remove the veins from the goose liver and wash, then soak in ice cold water for an hour. Finely chop goose fat and heat it in a pan. Remove the pieces and put aside the liquid fat.
Cooking: Drain the goose liver and place in a pot. Pour over the fat and enough water to cover. Season with salt, add peeled and crushed garlic and cook covered until a fork pricked into it comes out dry. Remove the lid and let the liquid evaporate. Brown both sides of the liver a little. Place it in a glass bowl, pour the fat over it and cool it completely. Keep it in the fridge.

Smoked goose sausage

1 large, fattened goose, (18-22 lbs / 8-10 kg),
1 packet pork small intestines, 3 tbsp salt,
2 tbsp paprika, 1 tbsp ground black pepper,
1 tsp icing sugar, 3 cloves crushed garlic,
half tsp ground cloves

Preparation: Carefully remove any remaining feathers and feather beds, cut it into pieces together with the skin and fat, and bone the meat. Put it through a grinder twice and knead the mixture well with the herbs. Let it rest for one night in a cool place, then knead again next day.

Cooking: Wash and soak intestines in lukewarm water until they are ready to be used and fill them with the meat mixture. Twist the intestines at 5 inches / 15 cm intervals, and cut them into pairs. Hang the pairs on a bar and let them air for a few hours. Have them smoked over cold smoke until they turn lovely and red. Wrap the sausages in absorbent paper and keep them in the vegetable drawer of the fridge. This way they will keep well for several months.

Smoked meat dishes

Baked ham

1.5 lbs / 600 g raw smoked ham,
2 cups dry red wine, 8 oz / 250 g mixed stock vegetables,
1 horseradish root, 1 onion, 1 bay leaf, half tsp ground black pepper;
milk for soaking the ham

Preparation: Soak the ham in the fridge for two days completely covered with milk. Soak an unglazed earthenware baking dish in cold water for half an hour before cooking time.

Cooking: Drain the ham and place it in the earthenware dish. Scatter all the sliced vegetables and chopped onion around the ham, add bay leaf, black pepper and pour in the wine. Add enough water so that the liquid will cover the ham. Cover the dish and start baking in a cold oven. Bake at a low heat for 15 minutes, then turn up the heat a little and bake the ham in a low-to-medium oven for 2.5 hours. Remove the ham from the liquid and turmix the cooked vegetables with the wine juices. Add 1-2 tsp grated fresh horseradish and mix well. Let the ham cool a little, slice and serve with the sauce and mashed potatoes.

Ham with tarragon

8 slices cooked, smoked ham, 2 oz / 50 g butter,
half cup each milk and cream, juice and rind of 2 lemons, 1 tsp flour,
1 tsp dried tarragon, sugar, salt and pepper to taste

Preparation: Heat the butter in a pan and brown the ham slices on both sides, remove from pan and set aside. Sprinkle flour into the melted butter and gently fry until it turns a pale golden color. Season with salt, pepper, add sugar, grated lemon rind and tarragon. Pour in milk and cream, and cook, stirring until it thickens. Add lemon juice, put the ham slices back into the sauce and let it boil for 2 minutes. Serve with rice or pasta.

Ham with prunes

1 lb / 400 g cooked, smoked ham, 8 oz / 250 g prunes,
1 cup sour cream, 2 oz / 50 g butter, 1-2 tbsp wine vinegar, 1 tsp flour,
2 crushed cloves, pinch sugar, salt and pepper to taste

Preparation: Soak the prunes in enough water to just cover them, add wine vinegar, cloves, salt and a pinch of sugar. Mix the sour cream with the flour.
Cooking: Cook the prunes in their soaking liquid for 5 minutes, add the sour cream mixture and let it boil until it thickens. Slice the ham and brown on both sides in the butter. Place ham slices in an ovenproof dish, pour over the prune sauce and bake it until it turns golden on top. Serve with boiled rice sprinkled with fresh parsley, or with potato croquettes.

    KNUCKLE OF HAM PAPRIKA

Sólet with smoked pork neck
(or ham)

(A pork variation on a Jewish-Hungarian bean dish)

1.5 lbs / 700 g uncooked smoked pork neck or ham,
1 lb / 400 g large dried beans, 1 large onion,
4 oz / 100 g pearl barley, 4 eggs, 2 tbsp lard,
2 cloves garlic, 1 tsp paprika, black pepper to taste

Preparation: The best utensil to make *sólet* in is an unglazed earthenware dish. Soak the beans, pearl barley and smoked meat overnight, then next day discard the soaking liquid. Mix the peeled and chopped onion and the crushed garlic with the beans and pearl barley, and pour this mixture into the pre-soaked earthenware dish.

Cooking: Create a dent in the middle of the bean mixture and lay the meat in the middle. Put the whole eggs around it. Sprinkle with paprika and pepper, pour over the melted lard and enough water to cover. Cover the dish and start baking in a cold oven, slowly increasing the temperature. Bake in at a low heat for 15 minutes, increasing the temperature to low-medium for 20 minutes, then bake the dish for three hours in a medium oven. Remove the cover and gently loosen the *sólet* with a fork. Peel the eggs and cut them in half. Slice the smoked meat across its fibers. Serve the beans topped with slices of ham and the boiled eggs peeled and cut in halves. (If the *sólet* is baked in a heavy iron skillet you have to preheat the oven. The water should come up to at least an inch above the beans. The skillet should be sealed with aluminum foil and not covered with its own lid!)

Note: *Sólet* is sometimes made with goose fat, smoked goose legs or breast. This is also a delicious version!

Smoked knuckle of ham
with savoy cabbage and quince

2 small smoked pork knuckles, 1 small savoy cabbage,
1 cup sour cream, 1 quince, 1 tbsp flour, 1 tbsp oil,
half tsp ground black pepper, pinch ground caraway, a little salt

Preparation: Soak the smoked knuckle in cold water overnight. Next day change the water and cook over a low heat until so tender that the bones slide out easily. Cut the meat into large cubes. Separate the leaves of the savoy cabbage, thoroughly wash them and let them drip in a sieve. Drop the leaves into boiling water for 3-4 minutes, drain and cool. Peel and core the quince, then slice it thinly.

Cooking: Wrap a piece of meat in each savoy cabbage leaf together with a few slices of quince. Oil a shallow ovenproof dish and lay the leaf parcels in it. Mix the flour, sour cream, caraway, salt and pepper with half cup of water and pour this mixture over the savoy cabbage parcels. Bake in a preheated hot oven until golden brown. Serve with cold horseradish sauce.

Smoked goose legs
with lentil purée

2 smoked goose legs, 1 lb / 400 g brown lentils,
half cup sour cream, 1 small onion, 2 tbsp goose fat,
1 tbsp wine vinegar, 1 tbsp flour, 2 cloves garlic,
a little sugar and mustard, half tsp paprika, salt to taste

Preparation: Soak the smoked goose legs overnight. Next day place them in a pot and pour in enough fresh water to cover. Cook over a low heat until the meat becomes very tender. Let it cool in its own cooking liquid, then bone and cut into large pieces.

Cooking: While the meat is cooking, prepare the lentil purée: cook the washed and pre-soaked lentils in enough smoked meat soaking liquid to cover them. Sauté the finely chopped onion and garlic in 1 tbsp of goose fat, mix in a little salt and paprika and add to the lentils. (Don't add too much salt because the smoked meat liquid is salty in itself!) Prepare a light, brown *roux* from 2 tbsp of oil and 1 tbsp of flour, add it to the liquid and flavor it with mustard, sugar and sour cream. Let it boil for a few minutes. Put the sauce into a liquidizer and whiz it until it becomes smooth. Pour the lentil purée into a deep serving dish and serve topped with the smoked goose pieces. Pickled grated horseradish is a good accompaniment to this dish.

Miscellaneous meat dishes

Roast duck with garlic

1 whole duck, 2 cups sour cream, 3 medium onions,
1 whole garlic bulb, 1 hot green chili pepper,
half tsp ground black pepper, salt to taste

Preparation: Cut the duck into portions, rub the skin with salt and pepper and put the pieces into a large baking tray.
Cooking: Scatter the peeled and quartered onions and half the crushed garlic cloves around the meat. Season the sour cream with salt and pepper and sprinkle it over the top of the duck pieces. Top it all with slices of hot chili pepper, cover with foil and bake in a preheated medium oven for 1.5 hours. Remove the cover and let the top turn crisp and golden brown. Discard the excess fat before serving this dish with potatoes and sautéed cabbage.

Goose legs in piquant sauce

2 medium goose legs, 8 oz / 300 g mixed stock vegetables,
1 cup sour cream, half cup dry white wine, 1 small onion,
2 tbsp goose fat, 1 tbsp flour, 1 tbsp prepared mustard,
2 tsp sugar, 1 tsp paprika, half tsp ground black pepper,
2 cloves garlic, 1 pinch each of ground yellow mustard seeds,
ground coriander, ground bay leaf, ground juniper berries,
salt to taste

Preparation: Peel and slice the vegetables. Brown the goose legs in the fat, remove from the pan and set aside.

Cooking: Brown the vegetables in the remaining goose fat, sprinkle with sugar and let it caramelize. Mix in the herbs and spices and lay the goose legs on top. Pour in two glasses of water and cook until tender. Once the legs are fully cooked, remove them from the pan and set them aside. Thicken the sauce with sour cream and flour, add mustard and crushed garlic. Let it boil for several minutes, add the wine and put it into a liquidizer. Bone and slice the cooked goose legs and serve with the sauce and bread dumplings.

Goose with horseradish

giblets of a large goose, half jar pickled grated horseradish,
1 cup sour cream, 1 tbsp flour, 1 tbsp / 20 g butter, a little sugar,
1-2 tbsp freshly grated horseradish, salt, pepper

Preparation: Cook the goose giblets in a little salted water. Drain, bone and cut into slices.

Cooking: Heat the butter and flour until it foams, then pour in the cooking liquid of the giblets together with the sour cream. Cook, stirring all the time until it thickens. Mix in the goose meat and the pickled horseradish, season with pepper and a pinch of sugar. Serve with boiled potatoes and grated fresh horseradish.

Lamb with tarragon and rice

(for 6)

2 lbs /1 kg lamb, 1 lb / 400 g mixed stock vegetables,
7 oz / 200 g rice, 1 cup sour cream, 1 large onion, 3 tbsp oil,
1 bunch each parsley and tarragon, 1 small lemon, salt,
sugar and pepper to taste

Preparation: Wash the meat, cut it into cubes and pat dry. Peel and finely chop the onion, parsley and tarragon. Peel and slice the vegetables. Sauté the chopped onion in oil, add the meat and brown the pieces on both sides. Throw in the chopped vegetables and add 1 glass of water. Cover and cook for approximately 40 minutes.

Cooking: Remove the meat pieces and set them aside. Pour in the rice and 1 large cup of water. Season with salt and pepper, mix in the parsley and the tarragon. Squeeze the juice of the lemon into the rice, together with the sour cream and a pinch of sugar. Mix well. Meanwhile bone the meat, cut it into slivers and return it to the pan. Mix well with the rice, cover and cook for a further 25 minutes. It is ready when all the liquid evaporates.

Lamb stew

1.5 lbs / 600 g boned leg of lamb,
4 oz / 100 g smoked bacon, 1 cup red wine, 1 onion, 2 tbsp oil,
1 clove garlic, 1 tbsp each paprika and salt

Preparation: Dice the meat, peel and finely chop the onion and the smoked bacon. Fry the bacon pieces until crisp, then set aside the crispy bits.
Cooking: Sauté the chopped onion in the bacon fat, remove from heat and quickly mix in the paprika. Pour in the wine and the lamb cubes. Season with salt, add the crushed garlic, and cook until tender. Serve topped with the crispy bacon bits with boiled rice or potatoes.

Pork knuckle with onions

1 large boned pork knuckle, 3 large onions,
4 cloves garlic, salt and ground black pepper to taste;
oil for frying the onions

Preparation: Clean, wash and pat dry the knuckle and rub it with salt. Wrap it well in a large piece of aluminum foil to prevent the juices from leaking out during baking. Crush the garlic, and mix it with 2 tsp of water.
Cooking: Put the wrapped knuckle into a baking tray and bake in a preheated hot oven for an hour and a half. Meanwhile peel and thinly slice the onions and fry the rings in hot oil until they turn crisp and golden. Remove the knuckle from the foil and cut slits into its skin. Rub it all over with the garlic paste and place it in an ovenproof dish with the skin side up. Scatter the fried onion rings around it, and brown in the oven for a few more minutes. Serve with potatoes and a green salad.

Soured lights

1.5 lbs / 600 g pork lights and hearts, 1 carrot,
1 parsnip, 1 cup sour cream, 2 tbsp flour, 2 tbsp oil,
1 small onion, 1 bunch fresh parsley, 2 cloves garlic,
1 bay leaf, juice of half a lemon, a thin sliver of lemon rind without
the white part, 1 tbsp vinegar, 1 tsp mustard,
pinch each dried marjoram and paprika, salt, sugar and
ground black pepper to taste

Preparation: Thoroughly wash the lights and hearts and boil them for a few minutes. Drain and start cooking again in plenty of fresh water. Season with salt and cook until half tender. Add the peeled and sliced vegetables and all the herbs and spices. Cook until tender, drain, set the cooking liquid aside. Cut the lights into strips.

Cooking: Heat the oil in a different pan, brown the flour, add the paprika and 2 cups of cooking liquid, mix well. Stir and flavor with the vinegar, lemon juice and rind, sugar and salt. Let it come to a boil and put the lights and hearts into the sauce, mix in the mustard and sour cream, and cook for a few more minutes. Decorate with lemon slices and more sour cream, and serve with bread or potato dumplings.

Rabbit leg with garlic

4 rear rabbit thighs, 1 cup cream, 2 tbsp flour, 2 tbsp oil,
4 cloves garlic, salt and freshly ground white pepper

Preparation: Wash and pat dry the meat and season with salt and pepper. Coat both sides of the rabbit legs with flour.

Cooking: Heat the oil in a large frying pan and brown the meat pieces on both sides. Pour in the cream and mix in half of the crushed garlic. Cook covered over a medium heat for approximately 25 minutes. Remove the lid, add the remaining garlic and boil until its juice becomes thick and reduced.

Note: You can also prepare this dish with grated onions instead of garlic. You can release the aroma of the onions very well by putting them through a garlic press.

SAUCES FOR MEAT DISHES

Spicy sour cherry sauce

1.5 cups / 3 dl pure sour cherry juice, 1 oz / 20 g butter,
1 tbsp flour, 1 tsp mustard, 2 cloves garlic,
1 pinch each ground coriander and cloves,
salt and sugar to taste

Preparation: Melt the butter and sauté the peeled and crushed garlic. Sprinkle the flour over and lightly brown.
Cooking: Remove the flour-butter mixture from the heat and pour in the sour cherry juice. Mix and let it cook until it becomes thick, stirring all the time. Add the spices, flavor with the mustard, salt and sugar. Serve with boiled beef or chicken.

Prune sauce

1.5 cups smoked meat cooking liquid,
(or one smoked meat stock cube dissolved in water),
4 oz / 100 g prunes, 1 cup sour cream,
1 oz / 20 g butter, 1-2 tbsp sugar, 1 tbsp flour,
half tsp ground cloves, half tsp salt

Preparation: Soak the prunes in water for 2 hours, drain and chop finely.
Cooking: Heat the butter with the flour until it foams, pour in the smoked meat cooking liquid and let it boil, stirring continuously. Add the chopped prunes, salt and cloves, and cook over a low heat for 10 minutes. Finally mix in the sour cream and boil together for 2 minutes. Serve with cooked ham or knuckle.

Rhubarb sauce

1 lb / 500 g rhubarb, 6-7 oz / 200 g sugar,
half cup cream, 1 egg yolk, pinch salt,
pinch ground cinnamon

Preparation: Clean and wash the rhubarb, let it dry. Chop the rhubarb into small pieces and cook in enough water to cover with a pinch of salt.
Cooking: Add the sugar to the rhubarb and cook until the pieces fall apart. Remove from the heat. Mix the egg yolk with the cream and add it to the cooked rhubarb, then mix, using an electric mixer. Do not allow to boil again! This is delicious served with boiled chicken or duck.

Horseradish sauce with rosehip

3 tbsp rosehip jam, 2 tbsp hot mustard,
2 tbsp freshly grated horseradish, half of a small onion,
pinch salt, 1 tsp lemon juice

Preparation: Peel and grate the onion or push it through a garlic press.
Cooking: Mix the jam with the mustard, horseradish and onion, season with salt and lemon juice. Serve with game, roast goose or duck. You can prepare a bigger quantity of this sauce, as it will keep well in the fridge for about three weeks in a tight fitting jar.

Tomato sauce

1.5 cups milk, half cup cream, 1 oz / 30 g butter,
1 heaped tbsp flour, 1 small tin tomato purée,
1 bunch celery leaves, 1 tsp grated onion, 1 tsp butter,
half tsp ground black pepper, salt and sugar to taste

PASTA PELLETS SHEPHERD'S STYLE

Preparation: Heat half the butter with the flour until it foams, pour in the milk and cook, stirring all the time until it thickens.

Cooking: Fry the tomato purée in the remaining butter and mix with the cream. Add half cup of water, stir until smooth and mix into the white sauce. Flavor with onion, pepper, salt and sugar. Cook for 5 minutes stirring continuously. This sauce goes well with any boiled or grilled meat or vegetable.

Mushroom sauce

5 oz / 150 g mushrooms, 1 cup sour cream,
1 small onion, 1 heaped tbsp flour, 1 bunch parsley,
1 clove garlic, 2 tbsp oil, half tsp ground black pepper,
salt to taste

Preparation: Sauté the peeled and finely chopped onion in the oil until pale golden. Add the cleaned and finely chopped mushrooms, season with salt and pepper, cook covered with a lid until soft, then remove the lid and cook for a few more minutes until the liquid evaporates.

Cooking: Mix the finely chopped parsley and crushed garlic into the mushroom mixture. Mix the flour with 1.5 cups of water and pour it over the mushrooms. Let it boil for at least 5 minutes stirring all the time. Add the sour cream, mix and remove from the heat. Serve with boiled and roast meat.

Garlic sauce

2 cups milk, 1 cup sour cream, 2 tbsp flour,
1 oz / 40 g butter or margarine, 6 cloves garlic,
half tsp ground white pepper,
1 tbsp bouillon powder or a stock cube

Preparation: Heat the milk. Melt the butter in a deep frying pan and sprinkle in the flour. Let it foam while stirring, add warm milk and cook over a gentle heat, mixing it with an electric mixer all the time until it turns into a smooth and thick sauce.

Cooking: Season with bouillon powder and pepper and let it boil for a few more minutes. Finally add the peeled and crushed garlic cloves and the sour cream. Let it boil again, stirring continuously. This is delicious eaten with any type of meat or steamed vegetable, boiled potatoes, pasta, or dumplings.

Sorrel sauce

8 oz / 250 g sorrel, 1 cup cream, 3 tbsp oil, 2 tbsp flour,
1 stock cube, salt and sugar to taste

Preparation: Wash and dry the sorrel, chop the leaves into thin slivers and sauté in hot oil. Pour in 1 cup of water and let it come to a boil. Add the stock cube and thicken with a water-flour-cream paste. Season with salt and sugar.

Note: This sauce is traditionally eaten with boiled potatoes and fried eggs.

Paprika sauce

2 oz / 50 g smoked bacon, 1 large onion,
1 cup sour cream, 1 tbsp paprika, 1 tbsp flour, 1 clove garlic,
salt and pepper to taste

Preparation: Chop the smoked bacon and the onion very finely.

Cooking: Fry the bacon and sauté the onion in the bacon fat. Remove from the heat for a minute and add the paprika, stirring continuously. Add the crushed garlic. Season with salt and pepper and pour in half cup of water. Mix well and let it boil. When it is smooth, mix in the sour cream and do not let it boil again. It can be served with any kind of dumpling, or boiled meat.

PASTAS AND PASTRIES

Savory pasta dishes

Dödölle

10 oz / 300 g potatoes, 7 oz / 200 g semolina,
8 oz / 250 g onion, approx. half cup lard, flour,
salt to taste

Preparation: Peel, wash and grate the potatoes. Add enough water to cover and let it boil. Add the semolina and cook, stirring all the time. Add enough flour to get a slightly sticky and runny consistency, mix well, let it cool and dry a little.
Cooking: While the dough is resting, chop the onion and sauté in the lard. Prepare a small baking tray by rubbing it with lard, drop portions of the dough with a tablespoon into the baking tray, sprinkle with the sautéed onion and fat and bake in a hot oven.

Puliszka (corn meal)

1.5 pints / 800 ml water, 10 oz / 300 g corn meal,
1 tsp salt

Preparation: Boil the water with the salt and slowly pour in the corn meal, stirring the mixture all the time to prevent the formation of any lumps. Cook for 15-20 minutes until it becomes so thick that it separates from the side of the pan. Cut out large dumplings from the mixture with a wet spoon and place them next to one another on an oiled serving platter.
Note: This can be eaten plain as a garnish to any type of goulash. You can also bake it layered with sheep's curd cheese and melted butter poured over the top. This way it will stand on its own and is lovely eaten with a salad.

Pasta pellets shepherd's style

1 lb / 500 g potatoes, 8 oz / 250 g pasta pellets,
4 oz / 100 g smoked bacon, 2 large onions,
1-2 green bell peppers, 1 tbsp paprika, 1 tbsp salt,
4 cloves garlic

Preparation: Peel and dice the potatoes. Chop the smoked bacon and the onions very finely, core and slice the green bell pepper.

Cooking: Melt the bacon fat in a large cooking pot. Add the pasta pellets, and brown while stirring all the time. Add the chopped onion and fry together for a couple of more minutes. Pour in three times as much water as the quantity of the pasta, season with salt, add the paprika and crushed garlic. Cook covered with a lid over a low heat for 15 minutes. Add the diced potatoes, mix well and cook until everything is well done. By this time almost all the liquid will have been soaked up. Remove from the heat, let it stand for 15 minutes and serve.

Note: This dish is ready when it is still moist but not watery.

Slambuc

1 lb / 500 g potatoes, 8 oz / 250 g large square pasta,
7 oz / 200 g smoked sausage, 1 large onion,
1-2 green bell pepper, 1 tbsp paprika, 1 tbsp salt,
4 cloves garlic

Preparation: Peel and dice the potatoes. Very finely chop the smoked bacon, slice the green bell pepper. Chop the onion, peel and slice the sausage.

Cooking: Fry the bacon in a large pot, add the chopped onion and fry together for 2 minutes. Add the broken-up pasta sheets, and brown them, stirring all the time. Add the sausage slices, potatoes and bell pepper. Flavor with paprika, salt and crushed garlic, pour in 2 pints / 1 liter of water, and cook covered over a low heat for 20 minutes. Stir and cook covered until both the pasta and the potatoes become soft and soak up the liquid. (If it is too dry, pour in a little hot water). Remove from the heat, let it stand for 15 minutes and serve.

Note: It is supposed to be moist but not watery.

Sweet pastries and cakes

Home-made thin filo pastry

1 lb / 500 g flour, 1 large cup lukewarm water,
1 tbsp / 20 g lard, 1 egg, 1 tbsp vinegar,
half tsp salt

Preparation: Mix the salt and vinegar into the water, add all the remaining ingredients and knead the mixture until it turns into a soft, elastic pastry. Divide it into four round parts.
Cooking: Place the rounds on a floured clean table cloth or large kitchen cloth. Brush the top with melted lard, cover it with a piece of aluminum foil and let it rest for 15 minutes. Roll out one pastry round very thinly and carefully slide your hands underneath it. Gently pull the pastry outwards. If you do not want to do this step you can just roll it out as thinly as possible. Place the filling of your choice on top, roll up the strudel and bake in the oven until golden. Repeat the same procedure with the other three dough rounds.

Puff pastry for strudel

1 lb / 500 g flour, 1 cup sour cream,
1 egg, pinch salt; 8 oz / 500 g flour,
7 oz / 200 g pork or goose fat

Preparation: Rub 8 oz of flour together with the fat and set aside. Knead 1 lb of flour together with the sour cream, egg and salt, then let it rest for 30 minutes.
Cooking: Roll out the egg pastry on a well floured wooden board and spread the fatty pastry over the top. Work the two pastries together then cut the result into six pieces. Roll out each piece into a large sheet the size of a baking tray, fill each one with a savory filling, roll them up, brush the top with egg and bake until golden brown.
Note: This pastry is thicker than the shop bought filo pastry variety.

Apple strudel

1 packet of ready made filo pastry (six sheets),
2 lbs / 1 kg cooking apples, 4-5 oz / 100-150 g granulated sugar,
4 oz / 100 g breadcrumbs, 4 oz / 100 g ground walnuts,
2 tbsp apricot jam, half tsp ground cinnamon, half cup oil;
1 egg to brush the top

Preparation: Wash and core the apples, and grate them without peeling. Squeeze out the apple juice into a bowl. (It makes a refreshing drink!) Mix the grated apples with the walnuts, apricot jam, cinnamon, and enough sugar to make a moderately sweet filling. Beat the egg.

Cooking: Damp a clean kitchen cloth and squeeze out any excess water. Lay it out on your work surface. Open the packet of filo pastry and take out half of the sheets. Keep the other half in the wrapping until they are ready to be used to prevent them from drying out. Brush each open sheet with oil and lay them on top of one another on the kitchen cloth. Sprinkle the entire surface with breadcrumbs. Place half the apple filling in a neat row at one end of the pastry sheet and carefully roll it up with the help of the kitchen cloth. Place the roll on a shallow baking tray. Prepare the second one in the same way. Brush the sides and tops of both rolls with a mixture of oil and beaten egg. Bake in a preheated medium oven until golden brown. Slice the strudel while it is still hot and serve sprinkled with a little icing sugar.

Marrow-poppy seed strudel

1 six-sheet packet of filo pastry, 1 lb / 400 g grated marrow,
7 oz / 200 g icing sugar, 4 oz / 100 g ground poppy seeds, half cup sour cream, 1 egg,
grated rind of 1 lemon, 2 oz / 50 g butter, pinch salt; 1 egg to brush the top

Preparation: Mix the ground poppy seed with the sour cream, beaten egg, lemon rind, icing sugar, and salt. Add the grated marrow, mix well and taste if it is sweet enough.

Cooking: Put three sheets of filo pastry on top of each other, brush with melted butter and beaten egg. Place the filling at one end in a row, roll up and place the roll on an oiled baking tray. Prepare the other roll in the same way. Brush both of them with melted butter and beaten egg, and then bake in a preheated medium oven until golden brown. Slice while it is still hot.

Tasty *gibanica*

2 4-sheet packets of filo pastry, 1 lb / 500 g curd cheese,
1 lb / 500 g peeled and grated apples, 2 cups sour cream,
7 oz / 200 g sugar, 4 oz / 100 g poppy-seeds,
4 oz / 100 g raisins, 4 oz / 100 g ground walnuts,
4 oz / 100 g melted butter or lard, 2 eggs, ground cinnamon,
vanilla sugar and grated lemon rind to taste;
butter or lard for the baking tray

Preparation: Rub the baking tray with butter or lard. Prepare the apple filling by stewing the grated apples with a little sugar, cinnamon and grated lemon rind. For the curd cheese filling break up the curds with a fork, mix with the egg yolks, sour cream, raisins and some sugar.
Cooking: Place the first two sheets of filo pastry at the bottom of the baking tray, brush it with the melted butter, sprinkle with half of the ground walnuts, sugar and some sour cream. Cover it with the next pastry sheet and half of the apple mixture. Next comes another layer of pastry followed by all the curd cheese filling. Cover the curd cheese layer with another sheet of filo pastry and spread the other half of the apple filling over the top. Pastry again, then walnut and sugar, pastry, poppy seed and sugar. Finish the layering with a pastry sheet and sprinkle the remaining sour cream and butter over the top. Don't forget to brush each pastry layer with sour cream and butter all the way through! Place it in a preheated medium oven and bake for 30-40 minutes. (If the top layer turns brown too quickly cover the baking tray with aluminum foil.)
Note: It is very, very delicious and easier to prepare than to write down!

Fruity milk loaf – *kalács*

1 lb / 500 g flour, 1.5 cups milk, 4 oz / 100 g raisins,
3 oz / 80 g butter, 2 oz / 70 g icing sugar, 1 firm pear,
1 cooking apple, 6 plumes, 2 sachets vanilla sugar,
1 tbsp / 20 g yeast, 2 egg yolks, half tsp salt,
half tsp ground cinnamon, half tsp grated orange or lemon rind,
half tsp ground cloves; 1 egg and half cup milk to brush

Preparation: Wash, peel and core all the fruit, and cut them into tiny pieces. Set it aside. Pour half cup of milk into a large mug, crumble in the yeast, and 1 tsp of sugar. Leave this mixture in a warm place for a while until it rises and foams. Sift the flour into a large mixing bowl, add the remaining sugar and washed raisins. Add the salt, create a small dent in the middle of the flour and drop the egg yolks in the dent. Thickly butter a large cake tin (long, round or ring shaped) and coat it with flour.

Cooking: Add the liquids and the yeast mixture to the flour and mix into a dough. Knead the dough thoroughly (if you use a food processor it will only take 8-10 minutes.) Check the dough by gently pushing it with your finger. It is ready when it immediately regains its original shape. Now push the fruit pieces into the dough. Place it in the cake tin. It is important that the dough only comes up about half way to the sides of the tin because it rises while baking and can 'overflow'. Let the mixture rise for at least an hour in the tin, then brush the entire surface with beaten egg. Bake in a preheated medium oven. You can check whether it is cooked through by inserting a wooden skewer: if it comes out clean the *kalács* is ready. At this point pour over half cup of hot milk and put it back into the oven for another 10 minutes. (This will make it light and fluffy.)

Note: You can prepare larger quantities of *kalács* dough, wrap it in cling film in 1 lb / 500 g batches and freeze it.

Traditional flue cake – *kürtős kalács*
(Makes approx 12-14)

2 lbs / 1 kg flour, 3-4 cups milk,
1 egg plus 3 egg yolks, 4 oz / 100 g icing sugar,
4 oz / 100 g butter, 1 oz / 30 g yeast, half tsp salt;
5 oz / 150 g butter for glazing, 5 oz / 150 g sugar,
4 oz / 100 g chopped walnuts

Preparation: Mix the crumbled yeast into half cup of lukewarm milk and a little sugar. Leave it in a warm place for about 15 minutes. Sift the flour into a large mixing bowl. Create a dent

Spring onion meat loaf with wine

in the middle, pour in the whole egg, plus the yolks, melted butter, sugar, salt and yeast mixture. Beat the dough until it bubbles, adding the milk in small batches. The result should be almost as firm as a bread dough. Cover and let it rise for 1 hour.

Cooking: Expert flue cake makers begin the process by first creating embers in the open air and brushing a wooden roller with butter. Once the dough is risen, cut off a 5 oz / 150 g piece, and on a floured board, roll it into a long strip of about a finger's width. Wrap this long strip around the wooden roller so that no gap remains in between the strips. Flatten the dough with your hand and start baking the cake over the embers by turning it around slowly. When it begins to turn a nice golden color, brush it with melted butter on all sides and sprinkle with icing sugar. The sugar will caramelize during baking and give a lovely rich brown color to the cake. The baking time for each cake is about 12-15 minutes. Shake off the ready cake onto a wooden board and sprinkle the top with sugar and chopped walnuts. Repeat exactly the same procedure with each cake.

Note: This is a traditional Transylvanian recipe that is very difficult to prepare without the proper equipment. The 1 foot 1 inch / 35 cm long wooden roller is approximately 3 inches / 10 cm in diameter, with a thin iron bar running through its middle. At one end there is a 3 inches/ 10 cm long support, at the other end 2 feet / 60 cm long iron piece for turning it around. Stacks of bricks are stood left and right from the fire and the turning spit is placed on these. If you would like to try this recipe at home without the traditional equipment you can bake 12 small plaited loaves from the dough, brushing them with butter and sprinkling them with sugar towards the end of baking time. Finally sprinkle with sugar and chopped walnuts.

Walnut-poppy seed *kalács*

For the dough: 1 lb / 500 g flour, 1 cup oil,
3 egg yolks, 1 tbsp / 20 g fresh yeast, half cup milk,
1 tsp sugar, pinch salt
For the walnut filling: 7 oz / 200 g ground walnuts,
7 oz / 200 g icing sugar, 1 sachet vanilla sugar,
2 oz / 50 g raisins, half cup milk

For the poppy seed filling: 7 oz / 200 g ground poppy-seeds,
7 oz / 200 g icing sugar, 2 oz / 50 g raisins,
1 cup milk, grated rind of 1 lemon

Preparation: Crumble the yeast into a small cup, pour over the lukewarm milk and mix in the sugar. Cover and leave in a warm place for 15 minutes. Meanwhile sift the flour into a large mixing bowl and create a dent in the middle. Pour the yeast mixture and eggs into the dent, add salt. Pour in the oil bit by bit and enough milk to get a medium soft consistency. Knead the dough well and place it in a floured bowl. Sprinkle some flour on top, cover with a clean kitchen towel and leave it in a warm place to rise until doubled in size.
Meanwhile, prepare the walnut filling: mix the ground walnuts and sugar into the milk, than add the raisins and vanilla sugar. Mix well. Prepare the poppy seed filling in the same way from the ingredients listed above. Cut the dough in half. Roll out each piece to 5 mm thickness and spread the walnut and poppy seed fillings over the entire surface of each piece. Roll them up and let them rest for another half an hour on the board. Carefully place them on an oven tray, brush the tops with egg yolk, prick a few holes into each roll and bake them in a preheated, hot oven. Let them cool completely before slicing.

Leavened curd cheese pie with dill

For the pastry: 1 lb / 500 g flour, 3/4 pint / 500 ml milk,
1 tbsp / 20 g yeast, 1 tbsp icing sugar, 1 egg, half tsp salt
For the filling: 1 lb / 500 g curd cheese, 1 cup sour cream,
3 eggs, 2 medium sized boiled potatoes,
3 tbsp sugar, 2 bunches fresh dill, half tsp salt;
1 egg for brushing; 2 tbsp lard for the baking tray

Preparation: Mix all the ingredients for the pastry and leave it in a warm place to rise until it has doubled in size. For the filling, grate the boiled and cooled potatoes and mix them with the curd cheese, beaten eggs, sour cream, sugar and salt. Prepare a baking tray by thickly coating it with lard.
Cooking: Spread the pastry into the prepared baking tray and spread the filling on top evenly. Sprinkle it with the finely chopped dill and bake in a preheated hot oven for 15 minutes.

[82]

(Place a little oven proof dish with water at the bottom of the oven to create steam.) Lower the heat to medium and continue baking until a skewer inserted comes out clean. Cut the pie into squares and serve.

Apple pie

For the pastry: 1 lb / 500 g flour, 1.5 oz / 40 g butter,
3 tbsp icing sugar, 3 egg yolks, 1.5 cups milk, pinch salt,
1 oz / 30 g fresh yeast.
For the filling: 3 cooking apples, 2 tbsp apricot jam

Preparation: Wash, peel, core and quarter the apples. Mix the crumbled yeast and 1 tbsp of icing sugar into half cup of lukewarm milk, cover, and leave it in a warm place for 15 minutes. Sift the flour into a deep mixing bowl, create a dent in the middle and pour in the frothy yeast mixture, the egg yolks, the icing sugar, salt and remaining milk. Add the melted butter and work everything together. Put the pastry into a floured bowl, sprinkle the top with some more flour, cover with a kitchen towel and leave it to rise in a warm place until doubled in size.
Cooking: Roll out the risen pastry on a floured board to 5 mm thickness. Cut the pastry into 1.5 inch / 5 cm by 3 inch / 8 cm pieces and leave them to rest for another 15 minutes. Brush each apple quarter with apricot jam and lay them on top of the pastry squares. Now wrap each apple piece in the pastry so that it is completely covered on all sides. Push the two ends in and roll up. Place the parcels on an oiled or buttered baking tray and bake in a preheated, medium oven over a small pot of steaming water. Brush the top with apricot jam. You may use apricot, pear, or 3-4 pitted sour or sweet cherries in place of the apples. Brush the fruit with a jam harmonizing in flavor.

Aranygaluska – Golden dumplings

For the dough: 10 oz / 300 g flour, 1 large cup milk,
1 tbsp / 20 g fresh yeast, 1 egg yolk,
2 oz / 50 g butter, pinch salt.
For the topping: 4 oz / 100 g ground walnuts,
5 oz / 150 g butter, 4 oz / 100 g sugar

Preparation: Dissolve the crumbled yeast in half cup of lukewarm milk and let it stand in a warm place until it becomes frothy. Mix it together with the flour, egg yolks, salt and enough lukewarm milk to get a soft, elastic dough. Now knead the melted butter into the dough, shape it into a neat, round piece and place it in a well-floured bowl. Sprinkle some flour on top, cover with a clean kitchen towel, and leave it in a warm place until doubled in size.

Meanwhile mix the ground walnuts with the sugar. Brush a baking dish with melted butter. Roll out the dough to a finger's thickness on a floured board and cut out small rounds. Fill the baking dish with a layer of dough rounds, sprinkle plenty of ground walnuts and sugar on top and pour a little melted butter over. Repeat these layers until all the dough gets used up. Stand a small pan of water at the bottom of the oven to create some steam, and don't turn on the oven until you start baking. Bake in a medium oven for about 35-40 minutes. Serve immediately while it is still hot, accompanied by a sweet white wine sauce.

For the white wine sauce you'll need 2 cups of semi-sweet white wine, 5-6 oz / 15-18 g icing sugar, 5 eggs, 1 tbsp flour, 1 small piece lemon rind, 1 pinch each ground cinnamon, cloves and salt.

Mix the spices into the wine and let it boil. Beat the egg yolks with half of the sugar, add flour, and slowly pour in the hot wine while mixing all the time. Do not let the mixture boil again with the eggs. Beat the egg whites with the remaining sugar until it forms soft peaks and carefully fold it into the egg yolk mixture.

Christmas poppy seed pudding – *mákos guba*

For the leaven: 3 oz / 80 g flour, half cup milk, 1 tbsp / 20 g yeast.
For the dough: 1 lb / 400 g flour, 4 oz / 100 g butter,
2 oz / 50 g icing sugar, pinch salt, half cup milk.
For the topping: 4 oz / 100 g ground poppy seeds, 5-6 tbsp honey

Preparation: Mix the crumbled yeast and 3 oz / 80 g of flour into the lukewarm milk, cover and let it rise until doubled in size. Work it together with the flour, sugar, salt, and enough lukewarm milk to get a breadlike dough consistency. Knead it well, sprinkle the top with flour, cover with a kitchen towel and leave in a warm place to double in size.

Cooking: Roll out the dough with your hands into long, thin rolls of a couple of fingers thickness. Lay the dough on a well buttered baking tray. Let it rest for half an hour and then bake in a preheated medium oven until golden brown. Separate the dough rolls and cut them into 1 inch / 2-3 cm pieces. Put them into a large sieve and pour boiling salted water over the dough pieces, letting them drain before layering them in a well buttered ovenproof dish. Sprinkle with ground poppy-seeds and honey. Bake again in a preheated oven for 15-20 minutes.

Note: This dough can be baked in larger quantities because once it dries out it can be kept for up to three months. If it becomes too dry you can pour hot milk over it before using. Let it soak up the milk, sprinkle it with ground walnuts or poppy seeds and sugar or honey. A time saving option is to use shop-bought brioche or croissants in place of this dough.

Potato *pogácsa* with plum purée

1 lb / 500 g potatoes, 1 lb / 500 g flour, 8 oz / 250 g lard,
half cup milk, 1 oz / 30 g yeast, 1 tbsp granulated sugar;
plum purée for the filling

Preparation: Crumble the yeast into the lukewarm milk together with the sugar and leave it in a warm place to rise. Boil the potatoes whole in their skin, peel and mash. Mix with the flour, lard, salt and yeast mixture. If the dough is too firm, soften it with a little milk, (It has to be elastic and easy to shape).

Cooking: Roll out the dough thinly and cut into small squares. Put a little plum purée on top of each square and fold it up carefully. Make sure the plum purée cannot leak out anywhere. Shape each dough parcel into rounds, place them on an oven tray and bake in a preheated medium oven until golden brown.

Corn *prósza*

8 oz / 250 g sugar, 7 oz / 200 g corn meal, 4 oz / 100 g flour,
4 oz / 100 g butter, 1 cup buttermilk, 2 eggs, grated rind of 1 lemon,
1 sachet baking powder, 1 tsp salt;
butter and breadcrumbs for the baking tray

Preparation: Carefully melt the butter without burning it. Butter a baking tray and coat it with breadcrumbs.

Cooking: Beat the buttermilk and eggs together, add the sugar, salt, grated lemon rind, baking powder, melted butter and flours. Mix until it becomes a frothy and smooth batter. Pour it into the prepared baking tray and smooth the top with a spatula. Put into a preheated medium oven and bake until it is cooked through and the top becomes golden brown. Serve cut into squares.

Forgácsfánk (Twists)

10 oz / 300 g flour, half cup sour cream, 3 egg yolks,
1 tbsp rum, 1 tbsp lemon juice, grated rind of 1 lemon,
pinch salt; oil for frying; 2 tbsp apricot jam,
1 tbsp icing sugar and vanilla sugar for serving

Preparation: Mix the egg yolks with the icing sugar and sour cream, add rum, lemon juice, salt and grated lemon rind. Sift in the flour and work the mixture together well.

Cooking: Roll out the dough thinly on a floured board. Cut it into strips of 1.5 inches / 4 cm by 3 inches / 10 cm with a floured dough wheel. Make indentations in the surface of the dough strips and fry them in plenty of hot oil. Place them on several layers of paper towels and sprinkle with vanilla sugar. Serve with hot apricot jam thinned with 2 tbsp of water.

Carnival doughnuts

1 lb / 500 g flour, 6 egg yolks, 1 oz / 30 g fresh yeast,
1.5 cups milk, 2 oz / 70 g butter,
1 tbsp sugar, vanilla sugar, pinch salt; oil for frying;
apricot jam and 2 tbsp rum for serving

Preparation: Crumble the yeast and mix it with 1 cup of lukewarm milk and 1 tbsp of sugar. Leave this mixture in a warm place until it foams. Sieve the flour into a large mixing bowl. Create a dent in the middle and pour in the yeast mixture, egg yolks, salt, vanilla sugar and the remaining lukewarm milk. Knead the dough thoroughly adding the butter last. Shape the dough into a round and place it in a floured bowl. Sprinkle some flour over the top of the dough as well, cover the bowl with a clean kitchen towel and leave it in a warm place until doubled in size.

Cooking: Place the risen dough on a well-floured board, roll it out to a thickness of half inch / 12 mm and cut out rounds with a floured tumbler or a large biscuit cutter, then allow these rounds to rest on the board for 15 minutes. Pour plenty of oil in a large pot and heat it. Put only a few doughnuts at a time into the hot oil because they will expand while frying. Fry the bottom of the doughnuts under a lid, then turn them over and fry the other side uncovered. Remove the golden doughnuts with a slotted spoon and place them on several layers of paper towels to dry. Sprinkle with vanilla sugar and serve with hot apricot jam thinned with a little water and a touch of rum.

Pancakes – *palacsinta*

12 oz / 300 g flour, 1 pint / 600 ml milk,
14 fl oz / 400 ml soda water or sparkling mineral water,
2 eggs, half cup oil, 1 tsp salt. (If you want to fill them
with something sweet use only a pinch of salt).

Preparation: Beat the eggs, add salt and milk. Sift the flour in and mix with an electric mixer. Add the soda or mineral water. Do not beat with the mixer anymore after adding the soda water. Add the oil and gently stir with a ladle. Let it stand for half an hour and stir again, adding more soda water.

Cooking: Make very thin pancakes using a non-stick frying pan. Since there is quite a bit of oil in the batter there is no need to oil the frying pan. Fill the pancakes with any filling of your choice, roll them up and lay them in an oven proof dish. Cover and heat for 10 minutes in a medium oven. You can make sweet ones with curd cheese, chocolate, chestnut purée or jam; or savory ones with meat, mushrooms, cheese or vegetables.

Breads and savory pastries

Potato-caraway bread

1 lb / 500 g boiled, peeled and mashed potatoes (net weight),
8 oz / 250 g wheat flour, 1 oz / 2 g fresh yeast, approximately 1 cup milk,
3 tbsp oil, 1 tbsp sugar, 1 level tsp salt,
1 tsp caraway seeds, half tsp wheat gluten

Preparation: Mix the crumbled yeast and sugar into half cup lukewarm milk and let it stand in a warm place until it becomes frothy. Sift the flour and gluten into a large mixing bowl. Create a dent in the middle and pour in the yeast mixture, oil, salt and mashed potatoes. Mix together and gradually add enough milk to get an elastic dough. Knead until holes appear in the dough (Which takes 8-10 minutes in a food processor.)
Cooking: Shape dough on a floured board into a long and thin loaf. Sprinkle with flour and let it rise, covered with a clean cloth, until doubled in size. Place on a prepared baking tray. Brush the top with water and bake in a preheated medium oven until golden brown.

Whole meal rye bread

8 oz / 250 g whole wheat flour with bran, 5 oz / 150 g rye flour,
4 oz / 100 g whole meal spelt flour, 3 oz / 8 g dried yeast granules,
2 cups water, half cup oil, 1.5 tbsp sugar, 1 tsp salt, 1 tsp gluten powder,
1 tbsp caraway seeds

Preparation: Put flours, sugar, yeast, salt, gluten and caraway seeds in a large bowl and mix. Create a dent in the middle and pour in half of the water and the oil. Work it together and gradually add more water to get a good elastic dough. Knead until holes appear in the dough. (It takes 8-10 minutes in a food processor.)
Cooking: Shape the dough on a floured board into an oval, sprinkle with flour, and let it double in size, while covered with a clean cloth. Place it on a prepared baking tray. Brush the top with water and bake in a preheated medium oven until golden brown.

Spring onion milk loaf with wine

1 lb / 500 g flour, 8 oz / 200 g goose fat, 1 cup dry white wine,
half cup milk, 2 eggs, 1 bunch spring onions,
1 oz / 20 g fresh yeast, 1 tbsp sugar,
1 tsp salt, half tsp ground black pepper

Preparation: Finely chop spring onions including the green ends. Dissolve the yeast and sugar in lukewarm milk and leave to froth in a warm place. Work together the flour and fat, eggs, yeast mixture, salt and pepper and enough wine to get a good elastic dough.
Cooking: Let it rise in a warm place until doubled in size. Divide it into three parts, then shape three long rolls out of each piece. Braid them together. This mixture is enough to make three loaves. Brush the tops with melted goose fat and bake until golden brown.

Layered savory strudel

2 packs filo pastry, 1 lb / 500 g curd cheese,
4 eggs, 1 cup sour cream, 1 large bunch each of fresh chives,
dill and parsley, 1 large onion, 1 clove garlic, salt to taste,
half cup oil

Preparation: Separate the eggs, and beat egg whites until firm. Chop the green herbs and onion very finely.
Cooking: Push the curd cheese through a very fine sieve, mix with the egg yolks, sour cream and green herbs. Add the onion, crushed garlic, and carefully mix in the beaten egg whites. Separate the filo pastry sheets. Oil a baking dish and put four sheets of pastry at the bottom, brushing each one with oil. Spread half the curd cheese filling over the pastry. Cover with four more sheets and another layer of curd cheese. Finish layering with a large sheet of filo pastry on top. Brush it with oil and bake in a medium-hot oven for 30 minutes or until golden brown. Let it cool, and cut into squares.

Pogácsa with cracklings

12 oz / 300 g goose or pork cracklings, 12 oz / 300 g flour,
3 egg yolks, 1 tbsp rum, a little sour cream, 1 level tsp salt

Preparation: Mince the cracklings and mix well with half the flour until you get a pastry texture, then set aside. Make another pastry from the remaining flour with 2 egg yolks, rum and sour cream. Knead until you get a medium soft texture that is easy to roll.
Cooking: Roll out the plain pastry on a floured board and place the other pastry with cracklings on top. Fold in the four corners of the plain pastry and roll out thinly again. (You will be rolling out the two pastries on top of each other.) Repeat this process of folding and rolling out three more times, leaving it to rest for ten minutes each time. For the final time roll out the pastry to half an inch thickness, and score the surface in both directions before cutting it into rounds. Brush the tops with the remaining beaten egg yolk, ensuring that it does not run down the sides, because this could prevent the *pogácsa* from coming up nice and high during baking. Bake in a hot oven until golden brown.

Cabbage pie

1 lb / 500 g puff pastry, 1.5 lbs / 800 g white cabbage, 4 tbsp potato flakes,
half cup milk, half cup sour cream, 2 eggs, 1 small jar capers, 2 fl oz / 50 ml oil,
plus oil for the pastry, salt, pepper and sugar to taste

Preparation: Wash and grate or very thinly slice the cabbage, sprinkle with salt and mix.
Cooking: Caramelize the sugar in oil, add the salted cabbage, cover and cook until soft, stirring occasionally. Mix the cooked cabbage with one beaten egg, milk, sour cream, capers and their liquid, and the potato flakes. Let this mixture rest for 10 minutes.
Meanwhile cut the puff pastry into two on a floured board, and roll out one half into a thin rectangular shape. Spread half the cabbage in a row along one long end of the rectangle. Roll up the pastry and lift it carefully onto a baking tray. Brush the top with beaten egg. Repeat this process once more. Put the pies into a preheated hot oven and bake for approximately 30 minutes. Do not open the oven door during the first 15 minutes of baking time because the pie will not be nice and high. Cut into slices while still hot.

SALADS AND PICKLES

Cucumber salad

*4 cucumbers (approximately 1.5 lbs / 800 g),
1 cup buttermilk (or sour cream), 2 cloves garlic,
vinegar, sugar and salt to taste, half tsp paprika,
1 pinch ground black pepper*

Preparation: Wash the cucumbers but do not peel them. Slice them very thinly or grate on the coarse side of the grater. Season with salt. After half an hour, pour a dressing of water, vinegar and sugar over the cucumber (not more than 1 cup), and mix in the crushed garlic. Leave it in the fridge to mature for one hour, covered with cling film. Portion it out and pour a little buttermilk on top of each portion. Sprinkle with paprika and black pepper.

Black radish salad

*1 lb / 500 g black radish, 1 large onion, juice of half a lemon,
1 tbsp honey, 2 tbsp mild oil, 1 cup buttermilk, salt to taste,
half tsp ground black pepper*

Preparation: Peel, wash and pat dry the radishes. First slice them very thinly, then cut the slices into matchsticks. Peel and cut the onion in the same way, mix with the radish and season. Cover and let it stand for half an hour.
For the dressing, mix the buttermilk with the lemon juice, oil, honey, salt and pepper. Mix the radish with the dressing thoroughly, cover and refrigerate for a few hours.

Onion salad with mustard

1 lb / 500 g onions, 1 cup sour cream, 3 tbsp oil,
1 tbsp prepared mustard, 1 tsp vinegar, salt to taste,
ground black pepper, sugar, a little ground nutmeg,
1 bunch fresh parsley

Preparation: Peel and finely chop the onions, season with salt and let them stand for half an hour. For the dressing, mix the sour cream with the vinegar, oil, mustard, sugar, pepper, nutmeg and finely chopped parsley. Pour the dressing over the onions, mix well, cover tightly and let it mature in the fridge overnight. It keeps well in the fridge without the sour cream, so larger quantities can be prepared and the sour cream added only as and when needed.

Hotchpotch salad

2 chicories, 1 small tight lettuce, 1 cucumber,
half white cabbage, 1 small endive.
For the dressing: *3 oz / 100 g smoked bacon,*
prepared mustard, vinegar, sugar and salt to taste

Preparation: Wash the lettuce and tear the leaves into smaller pieces. Separate the chicory leaves. Thinly slice and season the cabbage and cucumber. Put all the vegetables into a deep salad bowl and refrigerate. Dice the smoked bacon small and fry until crisp., then separate the crisp bacon bits and the fat. Mix the bacon fat with 4 tbsp of water, 2 tbsp vinegar, 1 tbsp mustard, sugar and salt to taste. Mix the cooled salad into the dressing and serve immediately.

Potato salad with onions

1 lb / 500 g salad potatoes boiled whole in their skin,
2 large red onions, 4 tbsp oil, half tsp each whole coriander
and mustard seeds, vinegar, salt and sugar to taste

Preparation: Boil 1 pint / half liter of water with the vinegar, salt and sugar. Add all the spices except the black pepper. Add the peeled and thinly sliced red onions. Let it boil again and cook for 3 minutes. Add the peeled and sliced boiled potatoes and turn off the heat. Let it cool completely, then drain, put into a salad bowl, carefully mix with oil, season with black pepper and cover tightly. Refrigerate for at least two hours.

Note: This keeps well in the fridge for up to three days.

Cabbage pickling in a wooden barrel

(Sauerkraut)

tight and healthy white cabbage heads,
salt (2% of the cabbage's weight), vine and sour cherry leaves,
bay leaves, vervain, whole black peppercorns,
caraway seeds, juniper berries, 1 piece of fresh horseradish,
a few quinces, green bell peppers, lemon

Preparation: First wash the wooden barrel several times with a strong jet of water. Remove the outer leaves of cabbages with a knife, and shred the cabbages using a cabbage slicer. Put a layer of washed and dried sour cherry and vine leaves at the bottom of the barrel. Pack the shredded cabbage tightly layered with salt, spices and thin lemon slices. Repeat until all the ingredients get used up.

Fermentation: Once the barrel is full, cover it with a clean, white linen cloth topped with a wooden disc weighted down with heavy basalt blocks. Leave it to ferment for about four weeks at 68° F / 20° C. The liquid that forms has to cover the cabbage completely. If not enough liquid is formed, add just enough salted water to cover the leaves. Keep the sauerkraut for a few more weeks in a cool place (such as a cellar), and remove the foam from the top. If the top layer gets too soft remove it before it spoils the rest. The leaves must be covered with liquid all the time. Sauerkraut is a good source of vitamins at winter time. (Small barrels can be bought for home use).

Pickled gherkins

(Leavened gherkins)

small pickling cucumbers, 1 large bunch dill (can be dried),
6-8 cloves garlic, 1 thick slice brown bread, salt

Preparation: Wash and soak the cucumbers in lukewarm water. Drain, discard the two ends and slash the skins. Test every one of them, since a single bitter one can ruin the whole jar. Keep cutting off more until you can no longer taste anything bitter. Place half the dill in the bottom of the jar and pack tightly with the cucumbers. Put peeled, whole garlic cloves in between. Place the other half of the dill and the bread on top. Boil water with 1 tbsp salt per 2 pints / 1 liter, and pour over the bread. Put a lid on the jar and place in the sun for 3-4 days to ferment. Drain and keep in the fridge in its own liquid. This will keep for several weeks. **Note:** These pickled gherkins are preserved without an acidifier, with lactic acid fermentation. Hungarian summer is impossible to imagine without them.

Pickled custard marrow

any amount of custard marrow (eggplant), 1 large bunch dry dill,
1 head garlic, 1 slice brown bread, salt to taste

Preparation: Wash, peel, seed and cut the marrows into large batons. Place half of the dill in the bottom of a big jar and fill the jar with the marrow batons. Put peeled whole garlic cloves in between. Place more dill and bread on top. Boil the water with 1 tbsp of salt per 2 pints / 1 liter. Pour enough simmering salted water over the marrows to cover. Cover the jar with a small plate or cloth and place in the sun to mature for 2-3 days. It is ready when the water turns cloudy, and it tastes identical to gherkins! Drain the marrow, put into smaller jars and pour over the liquid through a very five sieve. Cover it tightly and keep in the fridge. Chilled marrow or gherkin liquid, diluted with soda water or sparkling mineral water, is an excellent and refreshing drink.

Pearl onions
with ginger and tarragon

2 lbs / 1 kg pearl onions (tiny pickling onions),
1 bunch fresh tarragon leaves, half tsp each of ground ginger
and ground black pepper; vinegar, sugar and salt to taste

Preparation: Peel the onions and place them in a mild water-vinegar-sugar-salt solution and let it boil for two minutes. Drain and fill the jars with the onions, putting tarragon leaves in between. Taste the liquid and add more vinegar, sugar or salt if needed (It is supposed to be rather sour). Add the ginger and pepper and let it come to the boil again. Pour this liquid over the onions immediately. Cover tightly and let it cool in a dry steam. (Jars with the hot onions are wrapped in newspaper and blankets and left to cool for a day or two.)

Pickled beetroot

any amount of beetroot, 1 fresh horseradish root per 2 lbs / 1 kg,
5 cloves garlic, half tsp whole caraway seeds, vinegar, sugar
and salt to taste

Preparation: Clean the beetroot thoroughly with a brush under running water, and then steam them in a pressure cooker over a cup of water. Peel the beetroot while it is warm, and then grate it. Make a pickling liquid from water, vinegar, sugar, salt and caraway seeds, and let it come to the boil. Layer the grated beetroot, horseradish and sliced garlic in jars. Pour over the hot pickling liquid, cover immediately and let it cool in a dry steam.

Sweet red bell peppers
stuffed with cabbage

as many sweet bell peppers as you wish, the same amount of cabbage,
1 cup pickling vinegar per liter, 2 oz / 50 g sugar,
1 heaped tbsp yellow mustard seeds, 2 tsp whole coriander seeds,
a few whole black peppercorns, 2 tbsp salt

Preparation: Remove the outer leaves from the cabbage and slice them very thinly. Mix with 2 tbsp of salt per 2 lbs / 1 kg and let it stand. Thoroughly wash and hollow out the sweet peppers, wash them inside as well and let them dry with their open end downwards. Gently squeeze the salted cabbage and stuff it into the peppers. Put as many stuffed peppers as you can fit into a large, pot-bellied jar. Combine the vinegar, sugar, salt and water to a pleasantly sourish liquid, and let it boil. Add the spices, boil for 5 more minutes and pour over the stuffed peppers while boiling hot. Cover it tightly and let it cool. Keep it in a dark and cool place – it needs three months to fully mature.

INDEX OF RECIPES

Printed by Szekszárd Printing House, 2006